ICT 4 life

Terry Freedman   John Wasteney   Jared Wilson

Series editors:
Pam Counsell Chris Jones

Series consultant:
Ann Weidmann

PEARSON
Longman

Contents

How to use this book

The Pupil Book that you are reading and the digital ActiveTeach are partners. You can use the book to refer to in class while you work or discuss. You can use the ActiveTeach to open up a new dimension. The ActiveTeach looks like an electronic version of the Pupil Book, but it has a lot of extra material. You can launch digital files such as videos, games, presentations, spreadsheets and animations. These are sometimes called digital assets. You can also check how you are progressing in your assessment profile.

The ActiveBook at the back of this book includes all the digital files so you can continue work outside the classroom. It does not include your assessment profile. You need to be logged on in school to access this.

Each unit has a challenge:
- A video guide to collaborating safely
- Create an e-time capsule
- Help fight global warming
- An e-card system for your school

At the beginning of the lesson you can see what capability and techniques you will be learning. Once you understand these, you will be able to use them again and again.

The ActiveTeach has a glossary to help you understand new words. Click on words in bold to see a definition.

These are points that you will be assessed on. If you do these well, you will get better marks! Look out for the activities with stars by them – they tell you which points are being assessed!

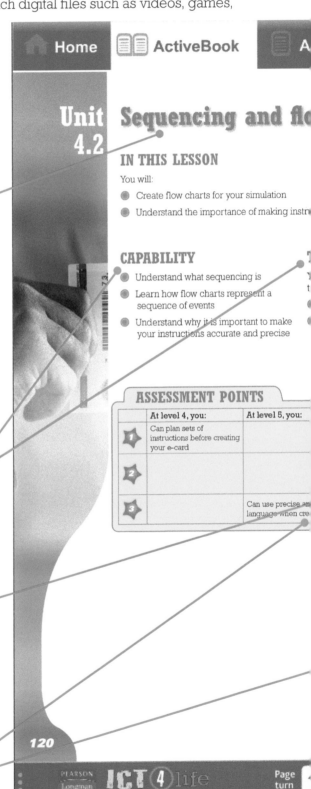

Home   ActiveBook   A

Unit 4.2 Sequencing and fl

IN THIS LESSON
You will:
- Create flow charts for your simulation
- Understand the importance of making instr

CAPABILITY
- Understand what sequencing is
- Learn how flow charts represent a sequence of events
- Understand why it is important to make your instructions accurate and precise

ASSESSMENT POINTS

	At level 4, you:	At level 5, you:
1	Can plan sets of instructions before creating your e-card	
2		
3		Can use precise an language when cre

120

PEARSON Longman   ICT 4 life   Page turn

The 'Assess' area contains the work you have done and the marks you have received. You can look at your profile to see how well you are doing and to identify areas that you need more practice in.

You can launch digital files (assets) from these tabs in the ActiveTeach. Each tab tells you what kind of file will be launched.

Go Online **Glossary** **Help**

An e-card system for your school Unit 4.2

:harts

Getting started...

Activity 1

▶ Look again at the video of people using different electronic systems.

● What order did they do things in? Complete these drag and drop activities.

● What would happen if you did things in the wrong order?

VIDEO

D+D

D+D

curate and precise

IQUES

arn or revisit the following

a flow chart

a flow chart

Let's go

Sequencing

Almost all systems use **sequencing**, or putting instructions in the correct order.

If you did the Gaming challenge in ActiveBook 1, you will have met the idea of sequencing before. Things happened in an order: for example, first the object hit a wall, then it made a noise and bounced.

At level 6, you:
Understand that complex information systems can be represented in a diagrammatical form in order to support their development

tions

Activity 2   Support

ASSESSMENT POINT

Remember, sequencing is about putting instructions in the right order.

▶ As a class, discuss the order of the step-by-step instructions you created for homework.

▶ Now discuss the order of the steps you wrote down. Does it matter what order they appear in?

Introducing flow charts

Flow charts are diagrams that help us to plan and show what order instructions should happen in, i.e. they show us the sequence of events.

Flow charts use special symbols which make it clear what is happening.

Try it out with the PIN system you created for homework.

The flow chart for this will look something like this diagram. The different shapes show what each step is about.

If the PIN is correct, it opens the menu screen.

If the PIN is not correct, it allows the user to try again.

WP

121

Use these controls to turn pages in the ActiveTeach – just like a real book!

5

The 'Can I do this?' demonstrations will help you learn and check the techniques you need as you work through the book. First you can see the technique demonstrated, then you have the chance to try it out.

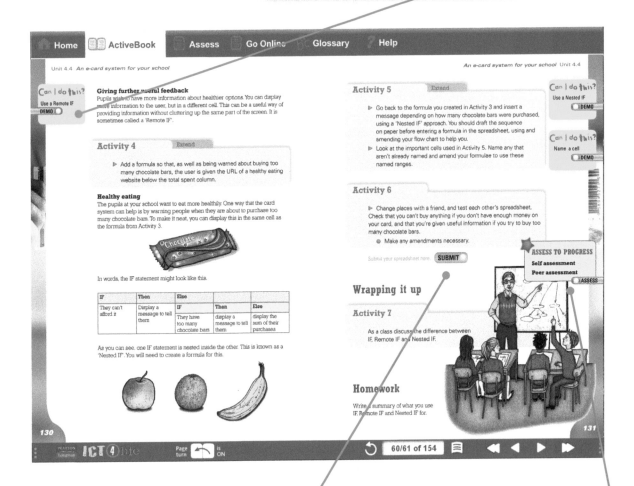

As you work, you will need to submit your work for marking. Click the submit button and browse to the file you want to submit. Your work will be stored in your assessment profile

When you've finished an activity, you can assess yourself (self assessment) by clicking on the ASSESS button in the ActiveBook and filling in the checklist. You can also assess a partner (peer assessment) by filling in the peer assessment checklist in their assessment profile.

Welcome to ICT 4 Life!

The story so far...

Firstly – well done! You have already taken some big steps to help you use ICT effectively in different situations, solving problems that you don't always know a lot about to begin with. This will help you to solve similar problems in future?

Why bother with ICT?

You use ICT every day; maybe you even have your own blog or create your own games. And now you can use these techniques to solve problems. So what's the point in continuing to learn ICT at school?

The truth is that technology is powerful and the only way to make the most of it is to learn about it and about how to use it properly. There are some crucial reasons why it is important to continue to study ICT in school:

- Before too long you will be presenting coursework for exams. It is very important to learn about different technologies so that you can choose the right one to present your answers as clearly as possible.
- You need to make the most of tools and technology, both new and familiar to you, so that you can make your work as effective as possible.
- Technology is powerful, but can also be dangerous to you or someone else if you do not use it safely.
- You need to use technology responsibly – we all know someone who has lost a lot of work through a virus or failing to save work properly.

What are the challenges?

In *ICT 4 Life 2*, you will meet new challenges which build on your knowledge, skills and understanding and allow you to make more of your own choices.

You will produce videos, websites, calculators and security systems, so you have the opportunity to show off what you can do – this isn't about boring exercises!

The challenge continues! Have fun!

Pam Counsell and Chris Jones
Regional Advisors for ICT

Unit challenge: A video guide to collaborating safely

Your tasks in this unit

Working in teams is fun and you do it all the time. You probably also work in small teams on school projects. Working together is called **collaborating**. But what if you needed to work with someone who lived in another town or country? That would make things more difficult. That's exactly why so many people use email, YouTube and similar technology – it allows people to collaborate even if they are not together.

In this unit, your challenge is to create a video for parents to tell them about collaborating digitally and why it is important.

Over the next eight lessons you will:

1 Explore examples of collaborative tools (including social networking tools)

2 Learn why they are useful (in school and out)

3 Discover what the dangers are

4 Understand how you can use these tools safely

5 Research how parents can help you with this.

The video should last no longer than two minutes and be suitable to put on the school website.

What are collaborative tools?

There are many, many collaborative technology tools. Can you recognise these?

Why are they useful?

On 30th July 2007 fans of the Harry Potter books took part in a live web chat with author JK Rowling. Readers submitted over 120,000 questions and many had their questions answered by their favourite author. Collaborative tools made it possible for fans to have a real-time chat with their hero, something they would not get the chance to do normally. This is just one example of how collaborative technology makes exciting things possible. Can you think of any more examples?

What do people think of them?

"MySpace lets me promote my band to lots of different people."
Aisha, Nottingham

"People will organise parties and I'll say 'I didn't know you were having one'. And they'll say: 'I put it on Facebook'. They forget that there's a real world out there."
Sam, London

"I worry about the people I meet online. How do I know they are who they say they are?"
Rhian, Caerphilly

"Emails are so much faster than letters and there's no paper so it's better for the environment too."
Ben, Aberdeen

"With photo sharing I can share photos with my cousins in America, it makes me feel closer to them."
Gurdeep, Hartlepool

"You need to be careful how much information you give out on social networking sites, my friend's birthday party was gate-crashed by some people who got hold of the invitation online."
Claire, Birmingham

What makes an effective video?

Look at these videos and think about these questions:

- Who is the audience for these videos?

- How well do they get their message across?

- What techniques do they use to promote their message?

Unit 1.1

Let's get together ...

IN THIS LESSON

You will:

- Discuss why you need to collaborate
- Find out how collaborative software can help you
- Start to use some collaborative software

CAPABILITY

- Understand how digital communications can be used to share information and communicate
- Select appropriate methods of exchanging digital information
- Consider the audience and purpose of your video
- Use digital communications to collaborate with others for a purpose

ASSESSMENT POINTS

	At level 4, you:	At level 5, you:	At level 6, you:
1	Know about the different ways of communicating digitally		
2		Can select the right method of digital communication for your audience and purpose	Are able to increase efficiency in a range of communications
3		Demonstrate that you know that digital communications can be used for the sharing and collaborative development of ideas	Are aware of the range of collaborative tools available to automate the sharing of information and communication

Getting started...

In this unit you will look at digital collaboration technology and produce a video to tell parents why such technology is important and how to avoid possible dangers.

What is collaboration all about?
It means working with other people. Why is that important?

Activity 1

- Brainstorm when it is important to work with other people and why.
- Watch this video with Ollie Bray, a **CEOP** Ambassador. How has digital collaboration been used in schools? Write down three advantages of using collaborative technology in schools.

Let's go

What tools do people use to collaborate?
It's always easiest to work together when you are face to face, but there are often times when that isn't possible. Technology allows people to collaborate even when they aren't in the same room.

How do people collaborate?

Activity 2

Extend

ASSESSMENT POINT

- ▷ Write down all the ways you can think of that people collaborate.
- Now think about the digital means of collaborating – what are the advantages and disadvantages of these? Make a list.
- What about other collaborative technology? You probably already use it socially or have seen others use it. How might it be useful for school work? Add to your list.
- How does this technology make communication more efficient? Can you make it do things automatically?

Audience and purpose

The purpose of the video you will create is to tell parents why **collaborative software** is important and how it can be used safely.

Think about your audience. How much do your parents know about collaborative technology? What do they think about **social networking sites**, **video conferencing**, etc.? You might need to explain the advantages of collaborative technology.

Activity 3

ASSESSMENT POINT

▶ As a class, look at your list of digital means of collaborating and select some you will include in your video to parents.

▶ Split into pairs and work on one digital means of communication each.

● Use a word processor to write down all the ways in which your digital communication could be used to work collaboratively.

● Write down the advantages and disadvantages of the digital means of collaboration you are working on. If you are not sure, you can do some research by visiting relevant websites.

● State clearly which **software** you have discussed and include your own names on the document.

Use collaborative software

You have all made notes on different software. You may need to use each other's work to create the video. You need to share it so that people have access to it. You will use some collaborative software. As you have just discussed, there are many different ways to share materials. Your teacher will explain the one(s) you will use.

Activity 4

ASSESSMENT POINT

- Your teacher will introduce you to the software you will be using to collaborate digitally. This might be a shared folder, email, your **VLE** or some other software.
- Add the documents you have just created to the collaborative area.

Now submit your notes here. **SUBMIT**

ASSESS TO PROGRESS

Self assessment

ASSESS

Wrapping it up

Activity 5

▶ As a class, discuss:
- the advantages and disadvantages of the digital tool you were discussing
- any problems with the shared area/software you used.

Homework

If you are not careful, there are risks involved in collaborating digitally. Think of, or research, a list of five potential risks.

Unit 1.2

Keep it safe

IN THIS LESSON

You will:

- Think about the risks of sharing information digitally
- Think about how you can avoid these risks and stay safe

CAPABILITY

- Understand the risks of sharing information digitally
- Work in a safe, responsible way when communicating with others

TECHNIQUES

You will learn or revisit the following techniques:

- Change browser security settings
- Identify a safe website
- Save your work

ASSESSMENT POINTS

	At level 4, you:	At level 5, you:	At level 6, you:
1	Know the risks of sharing personal information online and know what action you can take to protect yourself when working digitally	Know how to work in a safe and responsible way when communicating with others online	Are responsible, safe and secure in all communications
2		Can use automation to improve safety when using the internet	

Getting started...

Risks

Last lesson you looked at what collaborative software is and why it's useful. But a lot of fear has built up around this software. You need to look at the potential dangers of using it.

Activity 1

▷ Watch this video about the possible risks of collaborating digitally.

Let's go

There are dangers in communicating digitally. And people who get hurt are not stupid – they have just made a mistake. It can happen to anyone, but the danger is very real – people can be hurt very badly.

Online 'friends'

The great thing about digital communication is that you can talk to people miles away and find new friends. But some people are nasty and pretend to be someone else so that you make friends with them and trust them. But then they do things that can hurt you.

Activity 2

▷ Read these stories from real victims.
▷ Watch this video
   ● What did the young people do to stop the problem?
   ● How could they have prevented it in the first place?
   ● Could this happen to anyone?

Bullying

It isn't only people you don't know who can be nasty. So can people you do know. Bullying sometimes starts off as 'a laugh', but can really hurt other people.

Activity 3

▶ Look at this video and discuss:
- how the victim of bullying feels
- why you think the bullies are bullying them
- what the victim can do to help stop the bullying.

WWW

Inappropriate images and words

Sometimes people can send you things that you don't like. These messages or **postings** are known as **inappropriate**. Some software automatically filters out such images or will take down inappropriate postings when they occur.

Losing data

Putting your work in a place where other people can access it can also mean there are risks to your work. For example:

- Someone could delete the work by accident.
- Someone could change the work.
- Someone could copy the work and pretend it is theirs. Remember, this is why it is important to think about **copyright** when using other people's work yourself.

If you share files and attachments over the internet you are at risk from computer **viruses**. Viruses enter your computer system and delete files. You can protect yourself from most viruses by only opening files from trusted sources and installing virus protection software.

Personal information

People put all sorts of information on social networking websites without stopping to think of the thousands of people who might see it. **Identity theft** could be a problem for adults who put personal details like their mother's maiden name online because this is often used as a security check for banks. Companies are starting to search the social networking profiles of people who they are interviewing for work. It is possible in future that **data mining** will make it possible to pull together details of people held on various social networking websites now and in the past, which could potentially give a huge amount of information about an individual.

Activity 4

▶ Look at these three screenshots of someone's profile.
What problems do you think they might face?

IMAGE
IMAGE
IMAGE

Keeping safe

You've seen that there are dangers, but there are also ways of keeping safe.

Can I do this?

Change browser
security settings

DEMO

Identify a safe
website

DEMO

Activity 5

ASSESSMENT POINTS

▶ Split into groups and each take one of these dangers:
- online 'friends' who pretend to be someone else
- bullying
- inappropriate posting
- losing data
- personal information.

▶ In your group, open this planning document and write down a list of:
- ways to keep safe
- ways to use automatic settings in the software to keep safe
- what to do if you have a bad experience.

You can use these websites and demonstrations to help you.

WP

WWW
WWW
WWW

Save your documents, then upload them to your shared area so the rest of the class can access them.

Wrapping it up

Can I do this?

Save your work

DEMO

Activity 6

▶ Discuss what you have found out so far. Are there additional areas you should look at?

Homework

Continue to add to the planning document you started in Activity 5. Either add to a single planning document using the collaborative tools you are using, or bring your plan with you to the next lesson.

Unit 1.3

Plan it!

IN THIS LESSON

You will:

- Work in a **production team**
- Decide whether you will create an animation or a video of people
- Plan your video

CAPABILITY

- Analyse other people's work to understand what makes a video effective
- Plan your video and select the most appropriate form of video for your audience and purpose

ASSESSMENT POINTS

	At level 4, you:	At level 5, you:	At level 6, you:
1	Recognise common layouts and conventions used in video recordings and understand how they address the needs of your audience	Can assess video clips from other sources and use this information to help you plan your own video; you understand how effective videos meet your audience's needs and expectations	Use knowledge of publications and media presentation techniques to create complex success criteria to assess the quality and impact of your video and apply these to your own work
2	Can evaluate your work against simple, agreed criteria and understand how to improve it	Can make and use simple success criteria to ensure your video is fit for purpose	Can create and review complex success criteria to modify and develop your video as you go along
3		Can plan your video with consideration for audience expectations and your success criteria	Develop an understanding of technical considerations linked to effective and efficient digital communication

Getting started...

Activity 1

ASSESSMENT POINT

▶ Look at this video clip and answer these questions as a class.

- How does the video begin? What is it about?
- What do you know about the main characters? How do you know this?
- What camera angles are used and why?
- What is the climax of the film and how is it made effective?

VIDEO

Let's go

Success criteria

To help you plan your film, you need to think about what the success criteria are. Think about:

- the story – is it appropriate and interesting?
- how well the message is portrayed
- whether the characters and mood of the film interest the audience
- whether the camerawork is interesting
- whether the audio is appropriate
- how well your team has worked together.

Activity 2

ASSESSMENT POINT

▶ As a class, decide on your success criteria for your film.

Planning

Think about the audience for the video you will be producing, your parents. What subjects will appeal to them? What do they need to know? Remember: the video is to help them learn about collaborating safely, why it is important and how dangers can be avoided.

Your team

First you need to create your team. Divide into teams of about six to eight pupils. You will be working together to create your video, so it is important that you listen to each other and agree on your ideas. Your first task is to start your plan.

Activity 3
Support

ASSESSMENT POINT

▶ Start your plan by discussing and recording in a word-processing package:
- what the 'story' is – which messages are you going to focus on?
- who will be in it
- where it will take place.

Video or animation?

You must decide whether to video real people or create an animation of stills like Wallace and Gromit. Have a look at some of the techniques that can be achieved by each.

Filming techniques

These are ways of making the audience focus on something – the scene, the character, the emotion, the atmosphere.

Activity 4

▶ Look at these two photos:
How do you feel about the character?

When you are planning your video, you may want to include some filming techniques to add interest or to help the audience understand your characters or to focus on something in particular. These techniques include:

- Long shot – scene setting
- Medium shot – can see what is going on – interactions with people
- Close-up – focus on one character – expression
- Extreme close-up – focuses on character's emotions/reactions
- Oblique – can give a bizarre, worrying quality to the film

Take a look at this worksheet for more ideas on filming angles.

WP

Animation techniques

Animations are like cartoons, but they can sometimes deal with serious subjects. Look at this animation about bullying.

You will need **models** that you can move around. These don't need to be elaborate, they can be made from simple craft materials, cut-outs or Plasticine.

The techniques for video camerawork apply to animations as well, but bear in mind that it can take a long time. Each animation consists of lots of still pictures – **frames** – played one after the other very quickly. Standard animations run at 25 frames per second, so you would need 375 frames for a 15 second film! You will also need to think about file size when recording your images. So you need to make your message very clear and to the point.

Take a look at this worksheet for more ideas on stop-frame animation.

Activity 5

ASSESSMENT POINT

- ▷ As a team, based on what you have learnt, decide which type of film suits your plans best – video or animation.
- ▷ Write this on your planning document.

Submit your planning document here. **SUBMIT**

Wrapping it up

ASSESS TO PROGRESS

Self assessment

ASSESS

Activity 6

- ▷ As a class, discuss the ideas you have come up with and how suitable you think they are for your audience and purpose.

You need to get feedback on your ideas. Add your ideas to your collaborative area and/or email them to your parents or teacher and ask for their feedback on how suitable your ideas are for parents.

Homework

Encourage people to give feedback on your ideas. Record this and make sure you have it for the next lesson.

Unit 1.4

Telling stories

IN THIS LESSON

You will:

- Storyboard your video
- Use your collaborative software to get feedback on your storyboard
- Use this feedback to improve your storyboard
- Decide on roles within your team

CAPABILITY

- Structure your video to meet the needs of audience and purpose
- Use collaborative software to make your work accessible to others for the purpose of feedback
- Gather feedback on your work and use the feedback to improve your work, using success criteria
- Work efficiently, using automated tools available in your software, where appropriate
- Plan the roles that members of the team will perform

TECHNIQUES

You will learn or revisit the following techniques:

- Track changes

ASSESSMENT POINTS

	At level 4, you:	At level 5, you:	At level 6, you:
1	Know that the structure of your video presentation is important when meeting the needs of your audience	Can describe how information can be structured and sequenced to meet the needs of your audience	
2	Can evaluate your storyboard against simple, agreed criteria and understand how to improve it	Can make and use simple success criteria to ensure your storyboard is fit for purpose	Can devise and review complex success criteria to modify and develop your storyboard as you go along
3	Can make appropriate changes to your storyboard according to feedback	Can gather and use feedback to help you to plan your storyboard	Can gather, record and use systematic feedback from classmates to improve your storyboard
4		Can use digital communications for the sharing and collaborative development of ideas	Are aware of the range of collaborative tools available to automate the sharing of information and communication
5	Can use automated processes to keep the style and presentation of your video consistent	Can describe how to automate simple processes by using software tools to create your video	Know that existing systems can be refined and made more efficient through automation

Getting started...

Before you start filming, it is important to create a **storyboard**. This will help you to plan your video so that you don't forget anything and to make sure things happen in the right order.

Activity 1

▶ Look at this example of a storyboard. What does it help you to plan?

Shot	Description	People	Location	Camera techniques	Audio	Props	Duration
1	Long shot to introduce that film is about mobiles in school playgrounds. Key characters texting and laughing, surrounded by others playing.	Emily, Rohit and James, others in background	Football pitch	Long shot, panning	Introductory music, no dialogue that can be heard, just pupils laughing	Mobile phones	10 seconds

Let's go

Produce a storyboard

Activity 2

Support   Extend
ASSESSMENT POINTS ① ② ③ ④ ⑤

- In your teams, decide what your key messages will be for your **audience** of parents and how they will be put across in the film to achieve your **purpose**.

- In your teams, create your own storyboard template on your plan using suitable software or use the template provided.

- Now write your storyboard. Make sure to have enough detail in the description. Plan where you are going to film and check if this is possible. Write your dialogue in the audio column.

- Post your ideas to your collaborative area and ask for feedback from another team, remembering your success criteria. Ask them to make changes or comments so that they stand out from your text. There are many ways of doing this, some **automatically** which can be more **efficient**, depending on the software you are using.

- Look at the feedback and make appropriate changes to your storyboard.

WP

Can I do this?

Track changes

DEMO

Submit your storyboard here.   **SUBMIT**

ASSESS TO PROGRESS

Self assessment

ASSESS

Decide on roles

It is impossible for everyone to do everything, so you need to have roles within your team. For this film, roles might be:

- actors – acting the parts
- animator – moving the objects
- camera operator – behind the camera
- director – making sure everything happens as it should; thinking about how the film will look to the audience.

Activity 3

Decide on roles for each of your team. Remember, there may be more than one person playing each role, e.g. several actors. Equally, some people may play more than one role, e.g. direct the film, but also take on small acting roles. Note these down on your plan.

Wrapping it up

Preparation for filming

Activity 4

In the next lesson you will need to begin filming. Make sure:
- the location you have in mind is available
- the people you need are available and have learned their lines
- the equipment is available.

Discuss this with your teacher.

Homework

Gather together any props you will need, learn your lines, find any music you will use and plan your camerawork – you will not have long to film!

Lights, Camera, Action!

IN THIS LESSON

You will:

- Film your video

CAPABILITY

- Film your video according to your plan and checking your success criteria
- Use automatic camera settings to improve your work and make it more efficient

TECHNIQUES

You will learn or revisit the following techniques:

- Digital filming techniques

ASSESSMENT POINTS

	At level 4, you:	At level 5, you:	At level 6, you:
1	Show how your use of text, images and sounds can be changed and developed to improve your video	Can use appropriate text, sounds and images in your video	
2	Can match presentation and content to the purpose of your video	Can extract, combine and modify relevant information to improve your video	Can work independently and efficiently to combine information from a range of sources, structuring and refining your video for your specific audience and purpose
3		Can automate simple processes by using software tools	Understand that your video can be refined and made more efficient through automation

Getting started...

It's great to get down to filming, but before you go ahead, make sure you have agreed with your teacher:

- where you are going and who is going with you
- what equipment you are using
- how to use the equipment
- whether you should use any automatic features which may make your filming more efficient.

Also remember to have to hand:

- your storyboard and script
- your props
- your **success criteria**
- this book.

Take a look at this Can I do this? activity about tips on filming.

Can I do this?

Digital filming techniques

DEMO

Activity 1

▷ Discuss the points above and anything else you need to discuss with your teacher as a class.

Let's go

Activity 2

ASSESSMENT POINTS

▶ Record your film!
Once you have finished filming, make sure you store your video safely – check with your teacher the best way to do this.

Wrapping it up

Activity 3

▶ As a class, discuss how successful your filming was, what went particularly well and whether there were any problems.

Homework

Whether you have finished your filming or whether you are going to continue next lesson, you should make some notes while the filming is fresh in your mind so that you can work as efficiently as possible next lesson.

Write a list of the shots you think were the most successful that you would definitely like to keep in your video. Also write a list of shots you think were weaker and that you would like to delete.

Unit 1.6

Post-production

CAPABILITY

- Edit your video to make it fit for purpose
- Combine your video, audio and text to make an effective video
- Refine your video against your success criteria
- Compress your video to make it fit for purpose and more efficient to share
- Choose the right file type for your video
- Gain feedback on your video and use it to improve your work
- Work in a safe and responsible way when communicating with others

TECHNIQUES

You will learn or revisit the following techniques:

- Capture video
- Add zooms and effects
- Add transitions
- Add audio
- Compress and publish
- Edit a video
- Create stop-frame animation
- Add captions
- Save your work

ASSESSMENT POINTS

	At level 4, you:	At level 5, you:	At level 6, you:
1	Can use ICT to improve your video through drafting and refining	Can draft, refine and structure your video to get your meaning across effectively	
2	Show how your use of text, images and sounds can be modified and developed to improve your video	Can add appropriate text, sounds and images into your video	
3	Can match the presentation and content of your video to its purpose	Can extract, combine and modify relevant information for your video	Can work independently and efficiently to combine information from a range of sources, structuring and refining your video for its specific audience and purpose
4		Can use a range of ICT tools efficiently to refine your video	Identify the advantages and disadvantages of different software applications for your video and justify your choices
5		Understand that the format of the digital information impacts on the method of exchange	Can describe the technical limitations and strengths associated with a range of digital communication methods
6		Describe the implications of different means of digital communication for your intended audience and purpose	Know how to increase efficiency in a range of communications
7	Can act purposefully on feedback about your video	Understand the need to gather and use feedback to help improve your work in the future	Can gather, record and use systematic feedback from users to improve your work

Getting started...

Now that you have recorded your whole video, you will need to edit it. Editing involves cutting out all the bits of video you don't want, highlighting those that you do, and making sure the video meets your success criteria. In film-making, this stage is called **post-production**.

Activity 1

▶ As a class, discuss the types of changes you intend to make to your own videos.

Let's go

There are many different forms of video editing software and they can all do different things. But there are some key areas you should think about:

- How long does each shot need to be?
  As a rule, the scene should be as short as possible to portray the 'point' of the scene. Otherwise you may bore your audience.
- Which shots should I keep?
  Again, only keep the shots that really add to your message or point. Make the good and important shots stand out by focussing on them.
- What **transitions** should I use?
  Transitions, as in presentation software, mean moving from one shot to another. Take a look at the options on the demonstration.
- What audio should I include?
  Only include audio which is appropriate – the original soundtrack, music, background noise, sound effects.
- How big should the **file size** be? You will probably need to **compress** your files. Remember, your video needs to be suitable to include on a website.

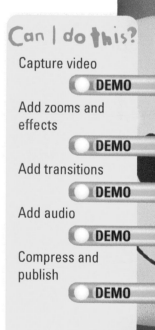

Can I do this?

Capture video
○ DEMO

Add zooms and effects
○ DEMO

Add transitions
○ DEMO

Add audio
○ DEMO

Compress and publish
○ DEMO

Activity 2

Extend
ASSESSMENT POINTS 1 2 3 4 5 6 7

Can I do this?

Edit a video
DEMO

Create stop-frame animation
DEMO

Add captions
DEMO

Save your work
DEMO

- If your teams are big, divide up into pairs. Each pair should save a separate copy of the video you have recorded. Now you can work on separate versions of your video.

- In your pairs, edit your video so that it is as effective as possible at meeting all of your success criteria.

- Post your videos to your shared area and compare with another pair from your group, or watch them together and discuss face to face.

- Make any suggested changes which you think will improve your video.

Submit your edited video here. **SUBMIT**

ASSESS TO PROGRESS

Self assessment

Peer assessment

ASSESS

Wrapping it up

Activity 3

▶ Discuss as a class:

- ● what you thought went well with editing your own video
- ● anything you thought effective about the other team's video you watched
- ● any problems you encountered
- ● how well you feel the messages about collaborating safely came across.

Homework

In the next lesson, you are going to look at how well you performed in this unit. In order to evaluate your work, you need to think about what you set out to do.

Answer the following questions:

- ○ What was the aim of the project?
- ○ What makes a successful video in this case?
- ○ What steps did you go through when creating this video?
- ○ What did you need to do to make sure your video was right for its audience and purpose?

Unit 1.7

It's a wrap!

IN THIS LESSON

You will:

- Evaluate your work and the work of others
- Enjoy your videos!

CAPABILITY

- Evaluate your work against success criteria and understand how you can improve future work
- Justify the choices you have made

ASSESSMENT POINTS

	At level 4, you:	At level 5, you:	At level 6, you:
1	Can evaluate your work against simple, agreed criteria and understand how to improve it	Can make and use simple success criteria to ensure your video is fit for purpose	Can devise and review complex success criteria to modify and develop your work as you go along
2	Can explain the reasons for the choices you have made in producing your video	Can justify the processes you have used to make your video	Can evaluate the effectiveness of your approach to making your video
3	Can choose when to use ICT to solve a problem	Demonstrate how reflecting on your work and learning can be used to improve your work in the future	Can apply your learning in future work

Getting started...

Congratulations! **It's a wrap** – you have finished your video! Not only should it look good, but it contains an important message.

Evaluate your work

Whether or not you are pleased with your finished video, it is important to evaluate your own work, and also to get ideas from other people on how you could improve.

Activity 1

▶ As a class, discuss the questions you answered for homework. What did you need to do to be successful in this unit challenge?

Let's go

Activity 2

ASSESSMENT POINTS

▶ Imagine you are submitting your video for a competition. Along with your actual video, you are asked to write a short report about how successful your video was. Make sure you answer the following questions:

- What was the aim of your video?
- Did you succeed in what you set out to do?
- How did you choose what you would do and why?
- Which software did you use and why?
- Which collaboration software worked the best?
- Did anything go wrong? Why?
- If you had more time, what improvements could you make?
- What have you learned about collaborating safely?
- What have you learned about producing a video?

It is also important to gain feedback from other people. When giving feedback to others, remember CHIPS!

Constructive If you didn't like something or it didn't work, say so, but say how it could be improved.

Honest Include things that didn't work. You will get credit for identifying the problem and proposing a solution.

Improvement Always consider what you would do to overcome problems and improve your work.

Proof If something is successful, give evidence in the form of specific examples.

Specific General points will not help anyone improve. You need to say exactly what was successful and what could be improved.

Activity 3

▶ Now post your video to your shared area or wiki and ask at least two of the people you worked with in this unit how they think you did.

Add the feedback comments you received to the report you wrote in Activity 2. Say whether you agree with the feedback you received.

Submit your self-evaluation report here. **SUBMIT**

ASSESS TO PROGRESS

Self assessment

ASSESS

Wrapping it up

Activity 4

Well done! Spend some time looking at each other's videos.

Homework

Next lesson, you will start a new challenge of creating an e-time capsule.

For homework:

- Write down what you think time capsules are.
- Imagine you find a time capsule hidden in your school. Write down what you would like it to contain.

Unit challenge: Create an e-time capsule

TIME CAPSULE
BURIED
December 29, 1999
TO BE OPENED
2100

Your tasks in this unit

A **time capsule** is a container filled with goods and information, and then buried. One problem with burying information is that over time the capsule may perish. Now you can solve this problem by using ICT tools to build an e-time capsule.

In this unit your challenge is to build and design an e-time capsule to be opened by people your age in ten years' time. The e-time capsule will be a website containing **multimedia resources** and information about what life is like today for people in your age group.

Over the next seven lessons you will:

1 Explore an example of an e-time capsule

2 Decide what material you want to include in your own time capsule

3 Design and build a website to host your time capsule

4 Add content and media elements to your website

5 Test and publish your e-time capsule

What goes in a time capsule?

Blue Peter Time capsule

On 7th June 1971 the presenters of childrens' TV programme Blue Peter buried the show's first time capsule in the grounds of BBC Television Centre in London. The capsule contained photographs of the presenters, some decimal coins – decimal coins came into use in 1971 – and a Blue Peter annual from 1970. In 2000 the presenters of the show dug up the time capsule after finding it using a map and thermal imaging equipment. There is one more Blue Peter Time Capsule buried in BBC Television Centre, it will be opened in 2050 and contains, amongst other things, an insulin pen and a France '98 football.

World's Fair Time Capsule

In 1939 at the World's Fair in New York a time capsule was buried to be opened in 6939 - 5,000 years' time! The capsule contents were selected to represent American life in 1939 and include fountain pens, a set of alphabet blocks, fabrics, metals, plastics, seeds, contemporary art, literature and news events collected on microfilm.

What does an e-time capsule look like?

Look at these e-time capsule websites and then think about these questions.

- What types of information are people saving in their e-time capsules?
- What are the benefits of using an e-time capsule instead of a traditional time capsule?

WWW

WWW

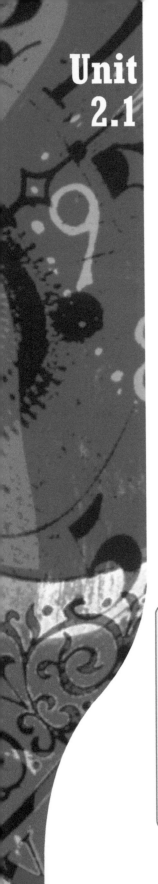

Unit 2.1

Who's it for? What's it for?

IN THIS LESSON

You will:

- Hear from a futurologist and learn how he predicts future trends
- Think about what you would like to include in your e-time capsule
- Begin planning the content for your e-time capsule

CAPABILITY

- Consider the audience for your e-time capsules

  Who is your audience? What do they need to know? Think about how old they are and what they might be interested in.

- Consider the purpose of your e-time capsule

  What is the aim of the e-time capsule? What is it trying to do?

- Plan your work to make sure it is suitable for audience and purpose

  Will your audience like your e-time capsule? Will it interest them? Will it fulfil its purpose? What software and tools will you use?

- Decide on what information you will include and where you will find this

ASSESSMENT POINTS

	At level 4, you:	At level 5, you:	At level 6, you:
1	Demonstrate that you know that information can be obtained from a range of sources	Can obtain information from a range of sources and assess its potential value	Can plan carefully for a range of information sources for an effective search
2	Can match presentation and content to purpose	Develop the ability to extract, combine and modify relevant information for your e-time capsule	
3	Can show how the structure of your e-time capsule is important when meeting the needs of your audience	Can structure and sequence information to meet audience needs	

Getting started

Activity 1

▷ Watch this video interview with Ian Pearson, a futurologist. As a class discuss:

- how Ian predicts future trends
- what Ian thinks life will be like in ten years' time
- how school life will have changed in ten years' time

Let's go

What is your challenge?

In this unit, your challenge is to create an **e-time capsule** in the form of a website. Your e-time capsule will contain **multimedia** information and **digital resources** that reflect what life is like for people in your age group today.

Your completed website will be locked away for ten years until another group of students of your age can open it and look at how life might have changed.

You have already learned quite a lot about creating presentations for other people – remember Sense of Audience and Purpose (SOAP) from last year.

In this unit you will think again about Sense of Audience and Purpose, but you will present your information in a very different format, a website. Websites both look and work very differently from most other forms of presentation.

Activity 2

▷ Click on the HTML tab and look through the website "BackinTime". Look again at the unit introduction.

In pairs or groups of three, discuss:

- why you think people like to look back at information from the past
- why you think predicting the future is difficult
- what aspects of your life will pupils your age in 2018 be interested in.

Where to start?

Now you know what you are going to produce, you need to think about who your audience is, why it is important and how you will produce it. You need to produce a plan.

Activity 3

WP

▶ Open this planning document and complete the first three boxes.

- What are you producing?
- What is the point of your e-time capsule?
- Who is the audience for your e-time capsule?

What information will you include?

The first stages in your planning are about what information you need to present in your website.

Activity 4

Support   Extend

ASSESSMENT POINTS

- Discuss with a partner what information you want to include in your website. Think about your audience and what they will be interested in. Fill in the next section of your planning document.

- Now think about the best way to present this information on your e-time capsule website. Is it text, a picture, a video, an audio clip? What will you need to think about? Fill in the next section of your planning document.

Where will you find this information?

It is important to think about where you will find the information you need so that you can plan whether you need to research it or create it yourself.

Activity 5

▶ Think about where you will find this information. Will you include facts you need to research and check? Will you video your own material? Fill in the next section of your planning document.

Wrapping it up

Activity 6

▶ As a class discuss some of the ideas you would like to include in your e-time capsule.

● Are they suitable for your audience?

● Are they likely to change in the next ten years, so your audience will find them interesting?

Add any additional ideas to your planning document.

Homework

In the next lesson you will evaluate some websites. Think of a website you have used recently and make a list of ways in which you thought the site was 'good' or 'bad'.

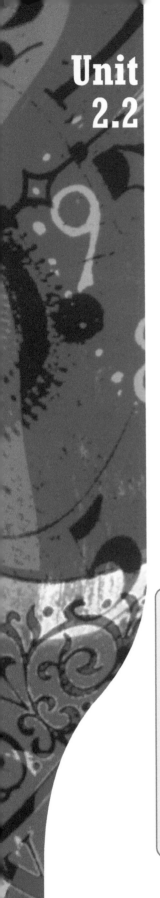

Unit 2.2

Catching a code

IN THIS LESSON

You will:

- Look at some code used in web pages
- Write some HTML code
- Discuss what makes a good and bad website
- Identify criteria for evaluating websites
- Create the success criteria for your own website

CAPABILITY

- Consider reliability of information sources and whether they are likely to be biased
- Look at other people's work and use your own knowledge of websites to develop appropriate success criteria
- Recognise common layouts and conventions used in different communications
- Recognise what formats are appropriate to a website

ASSESSMENT POINTS

	At level 4, you:	At level 5, you:	At level 6, you:
1	Can describe the difference between primary and secondary sources and the relevance this has to validity and bias		
2	Recognise common layouts and conventions used in different types of communication and how these address the needs of a familiar audience	Reflect on the work of others to help you plan your own communications; understand how effective presentations or publications address audience needs and expectations	Use knowledge of publications and media presentation techniques to devise complex success criteria to assess the quality and impact of communication products and apply these to your own work
3	Can describe some of the limitations and opportunities of different layout formats	Plan communication projects with consideration for needs of the audience, expectations, and criteria	Develop an understanding of technical considerations linked to effective and efficient digital communication

Getting started

In the next lessons you will make some changes to an existing website. This will help you to think about the format of your own e-time capsule. To be able to make these changes you need to understand a little bit about **code**.

Activity 1

▶ Open this website and select View and then Source. What do you see?

Try this again with the websites on page 39.

WWW

Let's go

What you have just seen is **HTML – HyperText Markup Language**, a code for web pages. This code provides the instructions for your browser to display the web page.

Computers use lots of different codes to make them work. They don't recognise letters, numbers or words the way you do. They use a different language called **binary code**.

Write HTML code

Activity 2

Now you're going to make your first website! To start, you need to open a text editor. Most computers have Notepad which is usually found in Program Files > Accessories.

● Open this document and type in the text, exactly as you see it, including the chevrons (< >).

● Save this file as myweb.htm in your folder.

● Close Notepad and look for the file myweb.htm in your folder.

● Double-click on the filename.

● What do you see? You should see your first web page!

WP

Evaluate websites

No one owns, controls or verifies the vast majority of information that you see on the Internet. Almost anyone can publish a basic website.

Deciding which sites to trust and which are not reliable is not always easy, but it is a key part of evaluating a website. When evaluating websites, think about the following key **evaluation criteria**:

C = **Coverage** – does the website cover the right information for your research?

O = **Objectivity** – factual sites such as encyclopaedias or news websites are reliable. Websites which are biased are mostly not objective.

C = **Currency** – is the website up to date? This is important so that you get accurate information.

O = **Origin** – who created the website? Are they reliable?

A = **Accuracy** – does the website generally seem accurate?

U = **Usability** – is it easy to use?

P = **Purpose** – is the purpose of the website to inform, entertain or persuade?

You might want to remember these evaluation criteria as **COCOA UP**.

Activity 3

ASSESSMENT POINT

▶ As a class, discuss each of the COCOA UP criteria.

Success criteria

Now that you have looked at what makes a good website, you should think about what will make your own website successful. You should think about:

- the audience and purpose of the website
- the information you will include
- the usability of the website
- accuracy
- how you will present the information.

Activity 4   Extend

ASSESSMENT POINTS

- Discuss your success criteria with a partner or as a class.
- Add your success criteria to your planning document.

Submit your planning document here. **SUBMIT**

Gather information

You need to start to gather together some information that you decided you would use on your website. Remember, if you use websites as a source of information, think about whether they are good websites using the COCOA UP criteria and don't forget to **acknowledge** your sources.

Activity 5

ASSESSMENT POINTS

▷ Start to gather information for your website. Some of your information might involve asking other people or using audio clips – you can continue this activity as homework.

Wrapping it up

Activity 6

▷ As a class, discuss:
- what makes a good website
- how you will make your own website good.

Homework

Continue to gather the information you highlighted in your planning document that you want to include in your website.

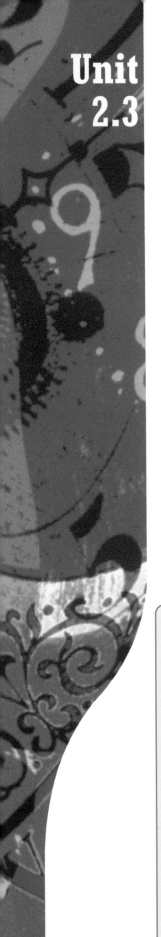

Unit 2.3 How will it look?

IN THIS LESSON

You will:

- Create a structure for your website
- Use the web software to amend your navigation automatically
- Start to develop your website by adding your information

CAPABILITY

- Modify and refine an existing site to meet certain criteria and a given context
- Develop your understanding of presentation in new media
- Automate the creation of navigation using software tools
- Consider how to collect and analyse data efficiently

TECHNIQUES

You will learn or revisit the following techniques:

- Use a text box
- Locate and open a website
- Use the Site tab
- Add pages
- Change the structure of a website

ASSESSMENT POINTS

	At level 4, you:	At level 5, you:	At level 6, you:
1	Use ICT to help to improve your work through drafting and refining	Can draft, refine and structure your work to convey meaning more effectively	
2	Understand how your use of text, images and sounds can be modified and developed to improve your work	Can incorporate appropriate text, sounds and images into your e-time capsule	
3	Can match presentation and content to purpose	Develop the ability to extract, combine and modify relevant information for your e-time capsule	Can work independently and efficiently to synthesise information from a range of sources, structuring and refining your presentation for specific audiences and purposes
4		Can automate simple processes by using software tools	Refine existing systems and make them more efficient through automation
5			Show that complex information systems can be represented in a diagrammatical form in order to support their development

Getting started

Structure a website

One of the most important parts of designing a website is structuring the information so that other people can find it. This is called **navigation**. First you need to consider what the key areas of information are – the **categories**. Then you need to provide a clear **route** to show users how to find that information.

Activity 1   Support

▷ Look at this website, which a pupil has started but not completed. This is the website you will be changing to become your e-time capsule.

As a class, decide what the key categories in this website are.

Think about the information you have been gathering for your website. What categories are there likely to be? Discuss some examples.

▷ Add these categories to your planning document. Try to have no more than three categories so that you don't run out of time in your lessons.

Let's go

Website diagrams

It is sometimes easier to decide how the navigation of a website will work by seeing it in a diagram. Look at this diagram of the website you looked at in Activity 1.

There are four key sections here which you should be able to get to from wherever you are on the website. These form the main navigation on the website. In the 'School' area, there are two sub-sections, but as these are not the main areas, they don't need buttons, just links from the 'school' page. Because this looks a bit like a family tree, these sub-sections are sometimes called 'child pages'.

Note that the homepage has the name 'index.html'. This is because 'index.html' is used as the **default** page in a website. So, for example, if you go to www.longman.co.uk, it will take you straight to the homepage. If you type www.longman.co.uk/index.html, it will take you to the same page.

HTML

WP

Can I do this?

Use a text box

DEMO

WP

Activity 2

▶ Draw a diagram in your planning document, using this template as a starting point if you wish.

ASSESS TO PROGRESS

Self assessment

ASSESS

Submit your planning document here. **SUBMIT**

Can I do this?

Locate and open a website

DEMO

Your working website

Now you need to change the navigation on the website to suit the information you want it to contain.

In order to make changes you need to rewrite the HTML code or use website creation software to make it easier. Many people now use WYSIWYG (What you see is what you get) software rather than writing in HTML code. The program lets you design your website as you see it, then turns it into HTML code so that it can be seen in web browsers. The examples in this unit use software called WebPlus and Dreamweaver. Your teacher will tell you which to use.

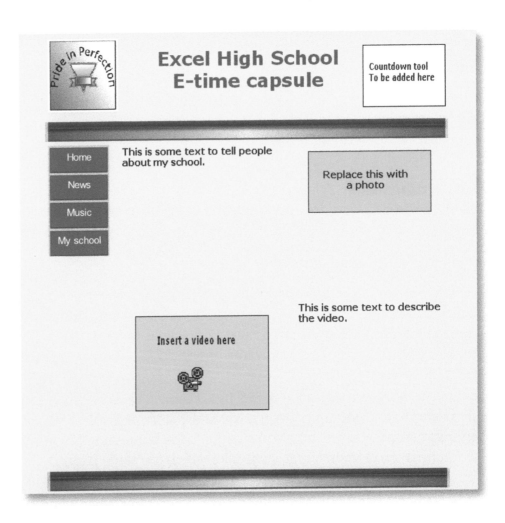

Activity 3

ASSESSMENT POINTS

▶ Make a copy of the relevant Excelhigh folder from the shared area and save into a new folder in your user area. You can rename it to an appropriate filename. Remember not to change the **file extension**.

● Open your WYSIWYG software and locate the Excelhigh website.

● Click on the Site tab (WebPlus) or file tab (Dreamweaver) to see the structure of the website. Discuss as a class how similar it is to the website you have planned.

● Watch the 'Can I do this?' activity, and then change your site to match the diagram you created in Activity 2.

● Note how the navigation changes automatically. Why is this a useful tool?

● Save your project and close down the software – you will continue using it next week.

Wrapping it up

Activity 4

▶ Look carefully at your planning document. Identify any elements that need:

● more research to find the information you need

● you to collect data or create information.

▶ Discuss as a class:

● when you will need to be aware of copyright

● whether you need to think about file sizes for content such as video or audio clips.

Homework

Continue to gather the information you highlighted in your planning document that you want to include on your website. Note which pages you will put this information on.

Can I do this?

Use the Site tab

DEMO

Add pages

DEMO

Change the structure of a website

DEMO

DW

WEBP

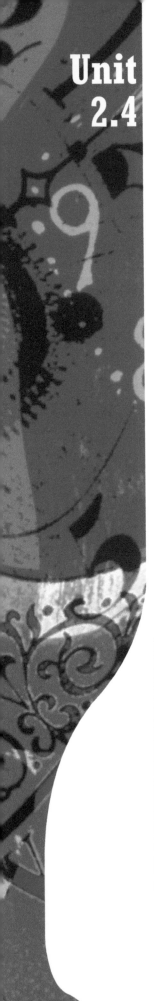

Unit 2.4

Making changes

IN THIS LESSON

You will:

- Consider what design and colour scheme is appropriate to your audience and purpose
- Make changes to a website's design to make it appropriate
- Use software tools to maximise efficiency and accuracy
- Add a video to your website

CAPABILITY

- Use your knowledge of websites to consider what is appropriate to your audience and purpose
- Make changes to design and layout to make it appropriate to audience and purpose
- Make changes efficiently and accurately by using software tools
- Add multimedia items

TECHNIQUES

You will learn or revisit the following techniques:

- Load and change features of the master page
- Preview page
- Add text
- Change font size and colour
- Insert an image
- Delete a web element
- Insert a Flash file

ASSESSMENT POINTS

	At level 4, you:	At level 5, you:	At level 6, you:
1	Recognise common layouts and conventions used in different types of communication and how these address the needs of a familiar audience	Can reflect on the work of others to help plan your own communications; understand how effective presentations or publications address audience needs and expectations	
2			Use knowledge of publications and media presentation techniques to devise complex success criteria to assess the quality and impact of communication products and apply these to your own work
3	Demonstrate that you are aware of some of the limitations and opportunities of different layout formats	Plan communication projects with consideration for needs of the audience, expectations and criteria	Develop an understanding of technical considerations linked to effective and efficient digital communication
4	Can use automated processes to support consistency of style and presentation, and describe the advantages of using automated processes	Can automate simple processes by harnessing software tools	Refine existing systems and make them more efficient through automation

Getting started

How will your website look?

You need to plan the look of your e-time capsule. To help you think about the sort of changes to make you will start to make some changes to the appearance, layout and content of an existing site and learn about the software that makes these changes possible.

Activity 1

ASSESSMENT POINT

▷ As a class, open the e-time capsule website in your browser. Discuss:

● which features are consistent throughout the website, e.g. school logo, colours

● which of these features you would like to change

● what would be appropriate to this website, e.g. school logo, colours.

Let's go

Efficient websites

You will not learn all of the functions of this software in a few lessons. However, you can soon learn the basics and quite quickly make a website that is fit for audience and purpose.

Most WYSIWYG web design software uses a system of **master pages** or **CSS (cascading style sheets)**. These are templates, much like the slide masters in PowerPoint. You can create basic colour schemes and certain web elements that will appear on each page. Every time you then add a new page, it will have those characteristics. It is an efficient way of building a website.

Activity 2

Extend

ASSESSMENT POINTS

- Decide which colours you will use – think about which colours are appropriate to your school and which will work well for the website.
- Watch the demonstration on how to load and change some features of the master page.
- Open the website you started to work on last week and select the master page.
- Choose a colour scheme. Remember the colours you use should make the website easy to use.
- Preview your amended page to check it looks right.
- If you are happy with your new colours, save your changes so far.

As well as the colours of a website, you can change the text and images on the master page.

Activity 3

ASSESSMENT POINTS

It is unlikely that your school is called Excel High School, so you will need to change the heading.

- Click the cursor into the Heading text box and change the name of your school. You may need to highlight the text and change the font size to make it fit.
- You will need to delete the image of the school logo and replace it with your school logo. Select > Insert picture and browse to find the image you will use. (Your teacher will tell you where to find this.)

Now that you have made these changes it is important to check if they work.

Activity 4

ASSESSMENT POINTS

- Check your work by previewing your amended page.
- Are you happy with your changes? If not, why? If you are not happy with the look of your site, make some further changes now.

Add video

You have already made some changes to the look and feel of your website by changing the title, colour scheme and logo.

You are now going to change the homepage to replace the video and add text to accompany the new video.

Can I do this?

Delete a web element

DEMO

Insert a Flash file

DEMO

Activity 5

ASSESSMENT POINTS

FLASH

- ▷ Open the page called Main.html.
  - Add the flash video clip of Ian Pearson talking the future.
  - Add your own brief text describing the video.

Wrapping it up

Activity 6

ASSESSMENT POINTS

- ▷ Discuss as a class the advantages of making changes to the master page.

Homework

Now that you know how to add text, images and video to your website, in the next lesson you will add your own content to the e-time capsule website. For homework, check that you have all the content you need and have it with you next lesson.

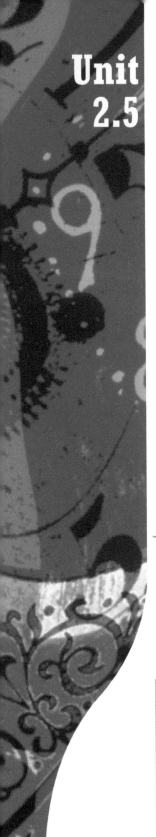

Unit 2.5

What's new?

IN THIS LESSON

You will:

- Add content to your website
- Add links to your website
- Add **media elements** to your website

CAPABILITY

- Incorporate information in the form of text, images and multimedia from a range of sources into the structure of your work
- Structure the information in your website appropriately and in a way that is suitable for audience and purpose taking account of technical considerations
- Link the information in a way that makes it easy to use and clear

TECHNIQUES

You will learn or revisit the following techniques:

- Load and change features of the master page
- Preview page
- Add text
- Change font size and colour
- Insert an image
- Add a video clip
- Insert a Flash file
- Optimise images
- Optimise videos
- Add hyperlinks
- Create an anchor
- Insert a web feed
- Copy a current web feed
- Use Paste Special
- Update a web feed

ASSESSMENT POINTS

	At level 4, you:	At level 5, you:	At level 6, you:
1	Demonstrate that you are aware of the variety of means by which communication can be exchanged digitally	Understand that the format of the digital information impacts on the method of exchange	Can explain the technical limitations and strengths associated with a range of digital communication methods
2	Use ICT to help improve your work through drafting and refining	Can draft, refine and structure your work to convey meaning more effectively	
3	Show that you understand how your use of text, images and sounds can be modified and developed to improve your work	Can incorporate appropriate text, sounds and images into the structure of a piece of work	
4	Can match presentation and content to purpose	Develop the ability to extract, combine and modify relevant information for a specific purpose	Can work independently and efficiently to synthesise information from a range of sources, structuring and refining your presentations for specific audiences and purposes

Getting started

Other web elements

Activity 1

▶ Look at this presentation about media elements on websites. Discuss as a class:
- how media elements can be a positive feature for a website
- how media elements can be a negative feature for a website.

Let's go

Add content

Activity 2

Now that you have collected your content, you need to add it to your website. Remember to:
- acknowledge any information that is not your own
- optimise your images and videos for web delivery (if the file size is too large, your web pages may take a long while to load)
- make your pages clear and easy to read.

Look at these 'Can I do this?' activities to help you.

Add links

As well as your navigation, you will need to link to other pages which are child pages of your main pages. You do this through adding a **hyperlink** to that page.

Activity 3

▶ Take a look at the demonstration activities and then add any hyperlinks or anchored links you think your website requires.

PRES

Can I do this?

Load and change features of the master page
DEMO

Preview page
DEMO

Add text
DEMO

Change font size and colour
DEMO

Insert an image
DEMO

Add a video clip
DEMO

Insert a Flash file
DEMO

Optimise images
DEMO

Optimise videos
DEMO

Can I do this?

Add hyperlinks
DEMO

Create an anchor
DEMO

Get up to date

The e-time capsule will be opened in the future, but your website is about the here and now. There are some web elements that can show what is happening now, such as the CBBC **RSS** newsfeed and a countdown tool. RSS feeds allow users to see when websites have added new content, a countdown tool is a feature you can add to a website to count down in real time to a selected date.

Choose one of the following options for Activity 4.

Either:

Newsfeed

Activity 4

ASSESSMENT POINTS

Some WYSIWYG software will allow you to insert RSS newsfeeds automatically. This activity requires you to have the full version of WebPlus. RSS feeds automatically update themselves each time the web page is loaded, but you need to set the static headlines for today so that people in the future can make a comparison on the day they open the time capsule.

- Insert a Newsfeed from this website.
- Now take a copy of this so that users in the future can see what the news was today. Add today's date.

Or:

Countdown tool

Activity 4

▶ This countdown tool is a **flash file**. To enable you to save it to your folder, it has been zipped. Save and extract the file and add it to your website.

Can I do this?

Insert a web feed
DEMO

Copy a current web feed
DEMO

Use Paste Special
DEMO

WWW

Can I do this?

Update a web feed
DEMO

Insert a Flash file
DEMO

FLASH

Wrapping it up

Activity 5

ASSESSMENT POINTS

▷ Discuss with your partner:

- why having an RSS feed on a web page might be a useful feature
- why you need to be careful about having too many media elements on a page
- why you should acknowledge the source of your web elements if they contain information not written by yourselves.

Homework

In the next lesson you will publish your website. Write down a list of three elements you will need to check before your website goes live.

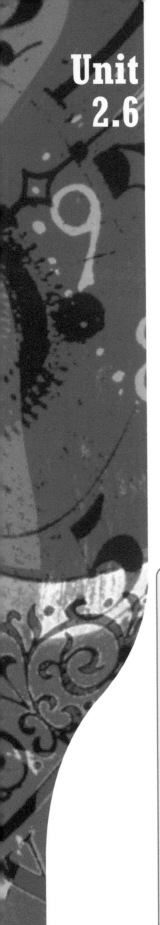

Unit 2.6

Get published!

IN THIS LESSON

You will:

- Check your website
- Test your website
- Publish your website

CAPABILITY

- Understand the importance of gaining feedback on your work and testing it to ensure accuracy and useability
- Improve your work as a result of feedback
- Choose an appropriate way to publish your website

TECHNIQUES

You will learn or revisit the following techniques:

- Preview page
- Add hyperlinks
- Add text
- Publish a website locally

ASSESSMENT POINTS

	At level 4, you:	At level 5, you:	At level 6, you:
1	Describe how ICT helps to improve your work through drafting and refining	Draft, refine and structure your work to convey meaning more effectively	
2	Understand the need to match presentation and content to purpose	Develop the ability to extract, combine and modify relevant information for your e-time capsule	Can work independently and efficiently to synthesise information from a range of sources, structuring and refining your presentations for specific audiences and purposes
3	Understand the need to select tools which will support the development and accuracy of your work and the benefits of checking, correcting and refining your work as it progresses	Can use a range of tools to improve the quality of outcomes for your audience and purpose	Explain how ICT tools can be used together to produce a variety of outcomes, enabling the most appropriate choice to be made
4		Can gather and use feedback to inform future work	Can gather, record and use systematic feedback from users to improve your work
5		Use reflection on your work and learning to improve your future work	Understand and demonstrate how to apply your learning in future work

Getting started

Web publishing

As you have been learning, websites need to be planned and designed.

Once the plans are in place the website is created either:

- by writing the design instructions in HTML code

or:

- by using some design software which lets you see how your page will look as you create it.

A finished website needs to be able to be viewed by lots of people. As people use different computers and different software we need software which will allow us to see our work, whatever we use. A **web browser** is software that can be used on any machine to display web pages.

The web browser only lets the audience view the web page; no one can edit the content from the web browser. So it is very important that the website is checked carefully before you **publish** it to the world.

There are various ways in which websites can be published:

- Websites are usually published to the Internet so they can be viewed on the world-wide web. To do this the website needs to be published to a special computer called a **server** that is permanently connected to the Internet and is open for people to use to access the published websites.

- Websites can be published to a local network – an **intranet** – so that only people on computers with access to the local network can view the website.

- Websites can be published to the hard drive of a PC or laptop and can only be seen on that one computer.

Activity 1

▶ As a class, discuss:
- when you might want to publish in these different ways
- how you will be publishing your own website.

Let's go

Check your website

Before you publish your website you should check that:

- all the information is there and displays correctly in the preview
- all the links and navigation buttons work
- there are no spelling mistakes.

As well as checking these things yourself, you should ask someone else to test them. There are several types of testing:

- Functionality – does it work?
- Usability – are the instructions clear? How easy is it to use?
- Improvements – what could I do to make it better?

In Unit 2.2 you created a list of success criteria for your completed website. You can use this list to help you to create a **test plan**. A test plan is simply a way of testing that a website works and does what it is supposed to do. Have a look at this example for ideas!

WP

WP

Can I do this?

Preview page
DEMO
Add hyperlinks
DEMO
Add text
DEMO

Activity 2

ASSESSMENT POINTS

▶ As a class, use the success criteria you created for your website and agree on your test plan.

- Create your test plan, based on this template.

Testing, testing, testing!

Now you have completed your test plan it is time to see if your finished website meets the success criteria.

Activity 3   Extend

ASSESSMENT POINTS

ASSESS TO PROGRESS

Self assessment
Peer assessment

ASSESS

▶ In pairs, preview your websites and your test plans.

- First test your own work, then each other's.
- For each of the test criteria, agree on whether or not they have been met and record this on your test plan.
- Make any necessary amendments to your website.

Submit your test plan here. **SUBMIT**

You will now convert your design into an actual website by publishing your work. You will publish your website to a new folder called MyWeb that you will create in your own school network area.

Can I do this?

Publish a website locally

DEMO

Activity 4

- Publish your website. You can use this 'Can I do this?' activity to help you.

Submit your website here. SUBMIT

ASSESS TO PROGRESS

Self assessment

ASSESS

Wrapping it up

Activity 5

ASSESSMENT POINTS **1 2 3**

▷ As a class, take a look at some of your websites. Think about:
- the different information you have included
- the different designs you have chosen
- which are the most successful features of the websites.
- the speed of downloads – are they fast enough?

Homework

Next lesson you will evaluate your own website. For homework note down:
- what went well with your website
- what didn't go so well
- how successful you think your website is.

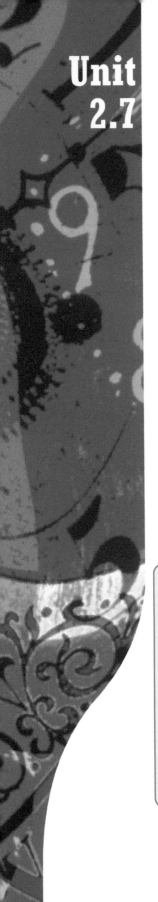

Unit 2.7 Judge for yourself

IN THIS LESSON

You will:

- Apply the criteria to evaluate your own website
- Apply the criteria to evaluate other people's websites
- Reflect on your learning in this topic

CAPABILITY

- Develop your understanding of developing and using criteria for evaluation
- Evaluate your own work and that of others against a set of criteria
- Be able to justify reasons for your choices and judgements

ASSESSMENT POINTS

	At level 4, you:	At level 5, you:	At level 6, you:
1	Can evaluate your work against simple, agreed criteria and understand how to improve it	Can make and use simple success criteria to ensure your website is fit for purpose	Can devise and review complex success criteria to modify and develop your website as it progresses
2	Can explain the reasons for choices you have made	Can justify the process you use in relation to the task	Can evaluate the effectiveness of your approach to developing an ICT solution
3	Can act purposefully on feedback	Can gather and use feedback to improve your work in the future	Can gather, record and use systematic feedback from users to improve your website
4	Can show that you know when to use ICT to solve a problem	Understand how reflection on your work and learning can be used to improve your work in the future	Understand and demonstrate how to apply your learning in future work

Getting started

Activity 1

▷ Open this document and read the question.

○ Why might you all have different answers to this question?

PRES

Let's go

It is important to evaluate your work against specific **criteria**. You saw in Activity 1 that unless you are specific, you can get very different answers.

When you evaluate, remember CHIPS:

Constructive   If you didn't like something or it didn't work, say so, but say how it could be improved.

Honest   Include things that didn't work. You will get credit for identifying the problem and proposing a solution.

Improvement Always consider what you would do to overcome problems and improve your work.

Proof   If something is successful, give evidence in the form of specific examples.

Specific   General points will not help anyone improve. You need to say exactly what was successful and what could be improved.

Activity 2

ASSESSMENT POINTS

▶ Look at the list of success criteria you created in Unit 2.2.

Write a short report on:

- how well your website meets these criteria
- what went well in your website and why
- what you weren't so pleased with and why
- what you would add to your website if you had time

Activity 3

ASSESSMENT POINTS

- Ask other people to check your website against these criteria. When it is your turn to give feedback, remember to give feedback on what is good as well as what could have been done better.
- Note the feedback on your report. Say whether or not you agree with the feedback.

Submit your report here. **SUBMIT**

ASSESS

ASSESS TO PROGRESS

Self assessment
Peer assessment

Wrapping it up

Now's your chance to look at each other's websites. Have fun!

Homework

Next lesson you will be helping to reduce global warming! For homework, find out about five problems which could be caused in the future by global warming.

Unit challenge: Help fight global warming

Your tasks in this unit

You have been asked by the Global Warming Agency (GWA), an environmental charity, to research the causes of global warming and to create an environmental calculator to help pupils work out their individual impact on the environment.

Over the next eleven lessons you will:

1 Research global warming and find out how humans contribute to it

2 Produce a spreadsheet model that pupils can use to calculate their environmental impact

3 Create a survey to collect people's opinions

4 Create a database to analyse the results of your survey

5 Compare your survey results with those of a recent national survey

6 Create a poster or leaflet to advertise your model

What are the consequences of global warming?

The rising sea levels could cause some animals' habitats to disappear completely.

Ocean water heats up causing reefs to die. Fish rely on the reefs for food so they die too.

The rise in temperature might cause some animals to become extinct.

Risks of flooding increase, putting homes and lives at risk.

What can you do about it?

Many people believe that global warming is the single biggest threat facing mankind and the planet, but not everyone agrees on how best to tackle the problem. There are hundreds of websites devoted to the topic of climate change so it's a good idea to read several websites and compare their content to get a rounded view. Here are a few to start you off:

Global warming   WWW

Effects of global warming   WWW

Carbon footprint calculators   WWW

Unit 3.1

What's causing global warming?

IN THIS LESSON

You will:

- Discuss global warming and the environment
- Use the Internet to find information on global warming
- Use keywords to refine your Internet search
- Record where you found all of your information and acknowledge your sources

CAPABILITY

- Choose keywords
- Search the Internet and reference your sources
- Use the advanced search facilities of a search engine

TECHNIQUES

You will learn or revisit the following techniques:

- Use search techniques
- Use the Alt-TAB function
- Use the advanced search facility

ASSESSMENT POINTS

	At level 4, you:	At level 5, you:	At level 6, you:
1	Can choose the right keywords to find information on global warming	Can select combinations of keywords to locate information on global warming that is useful	Can select combinations of keywords to locate relevant information on why global warming is occurring
2	Can alter your searches to narrow down the results you find when searching the internet	Can use logical operators in search engines and apply them in your search	Can make use of advanced Internet searches using logical operators when trying to narrow down searches
3	Describe why you should acknowledge the sources of information that you have gathered	Recognise how to correctly acknowledge sources of information found on the internet	

Getting started

Global warming – is it important?

Many people think that **global warming** doesn't affect them. Are they right?

Activity 1

Energy is all around
BUT
You need the right technology to make it useful

VIDEO

▶ Look at the unit introduction and watch this video from the Science Museum, then answer these questions:
  ● What effect does global warming have on you today?
  ● What effect might it have on you in 30 years' time?
  ● What causes global warming?
  ● Is there anything you can do about it?
  ● What is your 'carbon footprint'?

Let's go

Many people don't understand how important the **environment** is, and they often don't think there is anything they can do to help it. The Global Warming Agency (GWA), an environmental charity, has asked you to create a **model** to help pupils and their teachers and parents work out their environmental impact, or **carbon footprint**, and suggest ways to save energy.

Remember, models answer the question 'What if…?'. Your model will answer the question 'What if a person were doing things that cause global warming and how could they change their behaviour?' for lots of different people.

But first you need to find out exactly what activities cause global warming. You need to do some research.

Choose keywords

You have probably used Internet **search engines**, to find information on all kinds of different things. When you use search engines it is helpful to be able to find the information you need quickly and you can do this by making sure you choose the correct **keywords**. In the next activity you are going to use the Internet and keywords to find information about how humans are contributing to global warming.

Activity 2

ASSESSMENT POINT

Can I do this?

Use search techniques

DEMO

Before you start your search, discuss with a partner which keywords you think will help you to find accurate information about how humans contribute to global warming. When choosing keywords remember to think about the following:

- Do any of the keywords you have chosen have double meanings? Will they find what you are looking for?
- How will you find information that is easy to understand? This topic has lots of information for adults, but is there a way to find sites aimed at your age group?

Search the Internet and reference your sources

Now you have decided on your keywords, you will need to search for the information you need. When you search for information on the Internet, it is a good idea to record where you found the information. Remember:

- If you use any information you find on the Internet, you need to acknowledge it.
- Sometimes what you find may not be accurate or truthful, so choose your searches carefully! Think about who created the website and whether they are reliable, or likely to be **biased**.

Activity 3

ASSESSMENT POINT

WP

▶ Open your web browser and use your Internet searching skills to find information on why global warming is happening and reasons why people are damaging our environment. Complete the worksheet with your answers, showing where the information came from for each source you use.

Don't forget to save your work.

ASSESS TO PROGRESS

Self assessment
Peer assessment

ASSESS

Submit your completed worksheet here. **SUBMIT**

Can I do this?

Use the Alt-TAB function

DEMO

You may have two or more programs running, such as your web browser and a word-processing document. Why not use Alt-TAB to switch between them?

Advanced Search

You may have noticed that you are finding a lot of results in your searches and some of the web pages are not very useful. What you need to do is narrow your searches down.

Activity 4 — Extend

ASSESSMENT POINT 2

Can I do this?
Use the advanced search facility
DEMO

Use the **advanced search** facility in your search engine to narrow your search down. You can use this 'Can I do this?' activity to help you.

Select information

Once you have found relevant information, it is important to review it and select the information you really need.

Activity 5

Remember, the audience for your model is pupils and their parents and teachers. Look at the causes of global warming you have collected on your worksheet. Underline the causes that your audience is most likely to be able to affect. You can add more ideas of your own if you like.

Wrapping it up

Activity 6

ASSESSMENT POINTS 1 2 3

▶ As a class, compile a list of top tips for using keywords and Internet search engines to find information. Discuss any surprising or unusual results you found in your search. Did you always find the information you thought you would?

Homework

Now you need to think about the questions you will ask in your model. So, if you have underlined 'Travelling by aeroplane' in Activity 5, the question you will need to ask is 'How often per year do you travel by aeroplane?'

Using your list of causes from Activity 5, write a list of questions you feel you should include in your model.

Unit 3.2 Model behaviour

IN THIS LESSON

You will:

- Think about the things you need to include in your environmental calculator model
- Put together a list of success criteria for your model
- Consider what makes a good model
- Change an existing model to meet your needs

CAPABILITY

- Identify success criteria for your model
  What would you like your model to do?
  How will you know if it is successful?
- Assess your model against your success criteria
- Change your model to meet your needs

TECHNIQUES

You will learn or revisit the following techniques:

- Insert rows into a spreadsheet

ASSESSMENT POINTS

	At level 4, you:	At level 5, you:
1	Identify the success criteria for your model	Identify the success criteria for your model, understanding the reason behind the choice of software you will use
2	Understand that rules have to be created to make a model work	Understand that the rules operating in the model will affect the different output you see when you use it

Getting started

You can now start to plan your environmental calculator. This model will use the answers to your questions to calculate whether someone could change their behaviour to become more environmentally friendly.

How will you know if your model is successful?

Activity 1

▶ As a class, discuss the questions you wrote for homework. Listen to other people's ideas – they may help you. Think about how long people will have to work with your model and make sure you don't include too many questions.

Alter your list of questions if you want to.

Let's go

Success criteria

Now you have thought about what causes global warming, you need to make a list of success criteria for your model – what it should actually do! How will you know that your model has done its job?

Activity 2

ASSESSMENT POINT

▶ Put together a list of success criteria for your model. Consider:
  ● What are the key things that your model should do?
  ● How will you know if it is successful?
  ● How will you make it relevant to pupils, teachers and parents?

As a class, agree on success criteria for your own model. Open the calculator planning document and add your success criteria

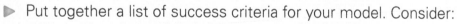

WP

Activity 3

▶ Look at this model and, as a class, discuss:

● What happens when you put in your answers?

● How does the model work out your feedback?

● Why has this particular **application** been used to make the model?

Assess a model

You should now have a good idea of what you want your model to do and the things it needs to include. You have been provided with an environmental calculator model that has already been started. Your challenge is to amend this model so that it meets your needs.

You need to assess the model against your success criteria so that you can see what you need to improve.

The model contains lots of **variables**. Variables are values in the model that can change – for instance, you can change the responses to the questions – these will affect the messages (**output**) you receive!

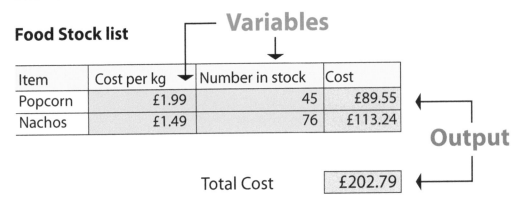

Showtime Cinema

Food Stock list — **Variables**

Item	Cost per kg	Number in stock	Cost
Popcorn	£1.99	45	£89.55
Nachos	£1.49	76	£113.24

Total Cost | £202.79 | **Output**

If we change a **variable** the **output** will change. In this case, we could change the **cost per kg** or **number in stock**, and the **cost** and **total cost** will change!

Activity 4

ASSESSMENT POINT

SS

▶ With a partner, open the environmental calculator model and try it out. Then discuss:

- what things you need to change (think about your success criteria)
- what elements of the model you think you should keep
- the links between the different variables and the output.

Write down these ideas on your calculator planning document.

Submit your calculator planning document here. **SUBMIT**

ASSESS TO PROGRESS

Self assess   **ASSESS**

Change a model for your needs

Now you have decided on the things you think you need to change, you will need to start building your own version of the model.

First you need to add in the questions you decided on in Activity 1.

Activity 5

▶ Save a version of the environmental calculator model to your work area with a relevant filename.

▶ Enter your new questions into the model.

Can I do this?

Insert rows into a spreadsheet

DEMO

Wrapping it up

Activity 6

▶ As a class, discuss which areas of the model you are going to change and whether you had any problems in inserting your new questions. Now look at the answers to the questions already in the spreadsheet. What do you notice about them?

Homework

Decide on the possible answers you will offer in response to the questions you added to the model in Activity 5. Write these down as you will need them in the next lesson.

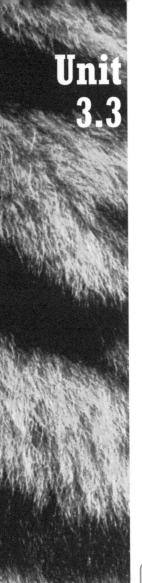

Unit 3.3

Get building

IN THIS LESSON

You will start building your environmental calculator. You will:

- Rate the environmental impact of different methods of travel
- Build your own model
- Amend the questions and answers in your model
- Create 'Lookup' tables to help you amend your model
- Learn how formulae can help you to add up the scores

CAPABILITY

- Assess an existing model
- Change your model to make sure it meets your needs
- Add your own functions to your model

TECHNIQUES

You will learn or revisit the following techniques:

- Use the 'Lookup' function
- Create an addition formula

ASSESSMENT POINTS

	At level 4, you:	At level 5, you:	At level 6, you:
1	Can say why your model will need different rules to make it effective	Can show that the rules in your model will affect the overall output	Can explain why the rules contained in your model need to be modified to use the information you have found from your research
2		Demonstrate that you can combine variables in your model to make rules	
3		Amend the rules in the environmental calculator that you have been given by altering the variables and the formulae	Create your own rules to add to the environmental calculator model to make it more effective

Getting started

Rate the environmental impact of different methods of travel

Activity 1

> You are going to travel from London to Birmingham. Each of the 'road signs' on the worksheet represents a way that you could travel. As a class, give each travel method a points score from 0 to 40 based on how environmentally friendly you think it is – with 0 being the best and 40 being the worst.

Now you have given different travel methods a score based on how environmentally friendly they are, you will need to do the same as part of your model.

Let's go

Activity 2   Extend

> For homework, you decided on the answers to your questions in your environmental calculator model. Discuss these with a partner to check that they are realistic.

Activity 3

> ▶ With the partner you have been working with:
> ● look at the list of answers in your model
> ● decide how many points each one should have.

Change your model to make sure it meets your needs

Now you have decided on the questions and answers in your model, you will need to start building your own version of the model. The first step is to look at some of the skills you will need to help you build this model.

Activity 4

ASSESSMENT POINT

▶ Have a look at this example of a **'Lookup'** table in action. Take a few moments to change the values it asks you to and then note down:

  ● what happens to the value at the bottom of the page
  ● why this is happening.

Once this is done, open your model and amend the questions and answers. Use the 'Look up' function to help you amend the spreadsheet so that you now have your own questions, a list of answers and your scores!

SS

Can I do this?

Use the 'Lookup' function

DEMO

Add your own functions to your model

To make your spreadsheet work properly, you will see that a **formula** has been used to add up the scores for the questions. This will allow your model to give users the messages you want them to see – you will learn more about these messages in the next lesson.

Activity 5

▷ Open your model, and watch what happens to the score when you change the answers. If you have added another question, you may need to amend your model so that it adds up the score for your new question. Have a look at this 'Can I do this?' activity to help you.

Can I do this?

Create an addition formula

DEMO

	A	B	C	D	E	F	G	H	I	J	K	L	M	N
SUM	▾ X ✓	=SUM()												

Environmental calculator

How do you get to school?   Car   10   Bus   5
                                                                       Car   10
                                                                       Cycle 0
                                                                       Walk   0

How many electrical gadgets...   1   0
                                                                       2   5
Function Arguments   ✕   3   10
SUM   more   20
  Number1 [   ] = number
  Number2 [   ] = number

=SUM()   Adds all the numbers in a range of cells.   =

Your impact   Number1: number1,number2,... are 1 to 30 numbers to sum. Logical values and text are
                            ignored in cells, included if typed as arguments.

Your environmental impact i: Formula result =

Environmental TOP TIPS   Help on this function   [OK]   [Cancel]

    Why not try walking or taking the bus?

Wrapping it up

Activity 6

▷ As a class, discuss why the functions you have used today are useful:

● How have they allowed the model to work?

● Have they made the model more user-friendly?

Homework

WP

Use the to answer the questions on simple formulae and 'Lookup' functions.

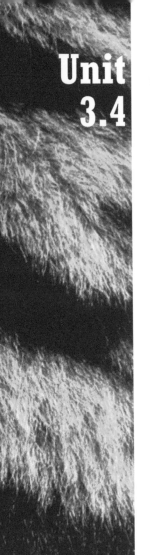

Add the magic formulae

IN THIS LESSON

You will add the finishing touches to your model. You will:

- Add functions to your model to enable it to deliver feedback to your participants
- Format your model so that it looks appropriate for your target audience

CAPABILITY

- Add your own functions to your model
- Format your model for your audience
- Hide unwanted data

TECHNIQUES

You will learn or revisit the following techniques:

- Use the IF function
- Change font, fill colour
- Adjust alignment
- Create borders and shading
- Insert an image
- Hide cells
- Use a text box
- Take a screenshot

ASSESSMENT POINTS

	At level 4, you:	At level 5, you:	At level 6, you:
1		Can combine variables in your model to make rules	
2	Can say why your model will need different rules to make it effective	Can show that the rules in your model will affect the overall output	Understand that the rules contained in your model need to be modified to use the information you have found from your research
3		Amend the rules in the environmental calculator that you have been given by altering the variables and the formulae	Create your own rules to add to the environmental calculator model to make it more effective
4	Format your spreadsheet model for your target audience	Format your spreadsheet model, showing an understanding of the needs of your audience	

Getting started

Activity 1

▷ Complete this weather worksheet as a class. Open the worksheet. Look at the weather condition and the statement and write down what you would do.

Let's go

Give feedback

On the model you have been given you can see that when people reach a certain score they are given feedback – usually a simple message. This is a useful way to show people what they have done right or what they have done wrong.

Activity 2

ASSESSMENT POINT

▷ Look at the message that is displayed on your model when you choose the answers to the questions you have now added. With a partner, discuss:

● which cells are changing
● when the message changes
● whether the message is appropriate
● whether more messages need to be added

IF the answer is...

The 'feedback' in this spreadsheet makes use of a combination of a simple formula and what is known as an **'IF function'**. An 'IF function' can be used to give a message when a cell meets a **condition** you have set and to give a different message if it does not.

The weather activity you did in Activity 1 works in the same way. If the entry is 'raining', the message would be 'take an umbrella'. For any other entry, the message would be 'take your sunglasses'.

IMAGE

Activity 3 — Extend

▶ Open this breakdown of a simple 'IF function'.

▶ You will notice that the function uses a symbol. You may have used these symbols in maths before. They are:

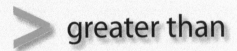

> **greater than**

< **less than**

▶ Amend your model so that your own message is shown.

Can I do this?

Use the IF function

DEMO

Format your spreadsheet

You have now added all of your formulae and functions to your spreadsheet. Next you need to make your model look good – remember that your audience for this model is people of your age, parents and teachers.

Activity 4

▶ Open your model and **format** it so that it looks appropriate for audience. Remember to think about your audience and what they will prefer. Think about the following:

- Colours
- Fonts
- Images
- Borders – to highlight areas for entering data

Can I do this?

Change font, fill colour

DEMO

Adjust alignment

DEMO

Create borders and shading

DEMO

Insert an image

DEMO

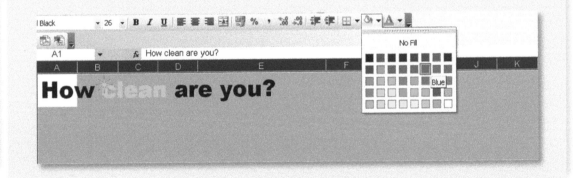

Hide and seek!

You may have noticed that some of the data on the spreadsheet models you have used could not be seen. These cells have been hidden so that users cannot access information you don't want them to see. This will make your model look much more professional.

Activity 5

ASSESSMENT POINT

Can I do this?

Hide cells

DEMO

▶ Open your model and hide the cells that you think should be out of sight to the user.

Don't forget to save your spreadsheet once you have finished. Take a **screenshot** of your model so far and paste it into a word-processing package. If necessary, print out the document to use for the homework activity.

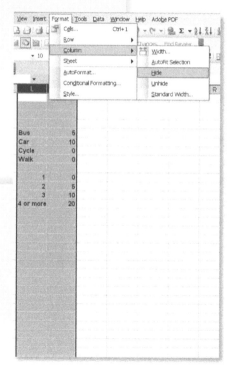

Wrapping it up

Activity 6

▶ As a class, discuss:
● how 'IF functions' can be used in your model
● where else 'IF functions' could be used in a model
● why formatting your model is important.

Homework

Either by hand on the printout or on screen using a text box, **annotate** the screenshot you pasted into your word-processing package earlier to show how you have formatted your spreadsheet so far to meet audience needs.

Can I do this?

Use a text box
DEMO

Take a screenshot
DEMO

Make it user friendly

IN THIS LESSON

You will learn about making your model user friendly. You will:

- Look at ways that computer based systems are made easy to use
- Make your model more user friendly

CAPABILITY

- Decide on ways to make a system user friendly
- Amend a model so that it is easy to use

TECHNIQUES

You will learn or revisit the following techniques:

- Add validation to a spreadsheet
- Add protection to a spreadsheet

ASSESSMENT POINTS

	At level 4, you:	At level 5, you:	At level 6, you:
1	Can say why your users may need help to enter data into your model, as they might enter the wrong values	Understand that the validation rules you create will help your model to give users the correct feedback	
2	Use validation and protection to make a spreadsheet easier to use	Can use validation and protection rules in your model to give feedback to users to allow them to understand what they are doing wrong	Create validation and protection rules for your model based upon your knowledge of what information people are likely to enter

IMAGE

Getting started

Activity 1

▶ Take a look at this data entry form.

As a class, discuss why the form is bad and what could be done to improve it

Let's go

Make it user friendly

User friendly is a phrase to describe something that is easy to use. Humans interact with machines every day. As a class, think of some of the machines you might already have interacted with today:

Were all of these easy to use? Successful machines should be easy to use because companies put a lot of thought into making them simple to operate. Why do you think being user friendly is so important? What do you think would happen if a PC or piece of software wasn't user friendly?

Activity 2

In groups of two or three, choose one of your spreadsheets to investigate and discuss:
- Is your model easy to use?
- What could you do to make it simpler to operate?

Validation

Validation is the process of ensuring that something you enter into a computer system is sensible or complete. For instance, some of you may have signed up for an e-mail or social networking account – do you remember how you entered your country or date of birth? Did you type this in or were you given a menu of choices?

Look at these two different images of validation in a spreadsheet.

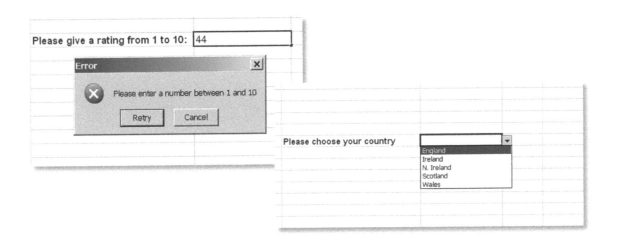

One of them prevents people entering invalid data by stopping inaccurate values, and the other gives users a menu of choices.

Which of these is most suitable for your model? Think about the following:

- If the answer is text, e.g. 'by bicycle', a menu of choices might be easier – otherwise you would have to think about all the possible ways of saying the same thing, e.g. 'by bike', 'cycle', etc.
- If the answer is a number, it might be just as easy for the user to enter the number but be stopped from entering inaccurate values.

Can I do this?

Add validation to a spreadsheet

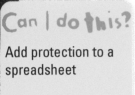

DEMO

Activity 3

ASSESSMENT POINTS

Decide which type of validation is most suitable and add it to your model.

Security

You have now almost completed your spreadsheet! But you may have noticed the fact that the users of your model can easily delete your formulae and other information – this isn't very good at all!

Many computer programs use **security** to stop users from altering or viewing data they should not – this is called **access control**. In a spreadsheet, this security is called **protection**

Can I do this?

Add protection to a spreadsheet

DEMO

Activity 4

ASSESSMENT POINT

You are now going to add some simple security to your spreadsheet. Open your model and add the protection. Because your teacher will need to access your work to see what you have done, you need to add the password 'ICT'. Once you have done this, save and print your completed model.

Submit your completed model here. **SUBMIT**

ASSESS TO PROGRESS

Self assess   **ASSESS**
Peer assessment

Wrapping it up

Activity 5

As a class, discuss:
- why and where validation is used
- why security is needed on computer systems.

Homework

On a printout of your spreadsheet annotate:
- where you have added validation to the spreadsheet
- why this has been added.

Unit 3.6

Start testing

IN THIS LESSON

You will:

- Create a test plan to test your model
- Test your model to make sure that it works

CAPABILITY

- Create a test plan
- Test your model
- Collect feedback

ASSESSMENT POINTS

	At level 4, you:	At level 5, you:	At level 6, you:
⭐	Use success criteria to test your model	Create a test plan to test that your model does what it is supposed to do	Use your test plan to test that your model works correctly, making any changes that you think are necessary

Getting started

Activity 1 — Extend

It is important to test a computer system and software thoroughly. There are several types of testing:

- Functionality – does it work?
- Usability – are the instructions clear? How easy is it to use?
- Improvements – what could I do to make it better?

As a class, discuss why you think testing is important and what things you might look for when you test your model. Discuss why functionality, usability and improvements are important.

Let's go

What to test?

In Unit 3.2 you created a list of 'success criteria' for your completed model. These were the things that your model *should* do. You can use this list to help you create a **test plan**.

A test plan is simply a way of testing that a **system** works and does what it is supposed to do. Have a look at this example for ideas!

WP

Activity 2

As a class, use the success criteria you created for your model and agree a list of success criteria for your test plan.

Create the test plan

Now you have agreed on what would make your model successful, it is time to create the test plan that you will use for your model.

Activity 3

Using the template you have been given, create a test plan for your spreadsheet model.

Testing, testing!

Now you have completed your test plan it is time to see if your completed spreadsheet meets the success criteria.

Activity 4   Extend

▶ In pairs, open your spreadsheet models and your test plans. For each of the test criteria, agree on whether or not they have been met and record this on your test plan.

Submit your test plan here. **SUBMIT**

ASSESS TO PROGRESS

Peer assessment
Ask the partner who gave you feedback to complete the peer assessment checklist in your assessment profile.

Make improvements

There is no point in testing your model if you do nothing about it! If you found that your model did not meet the test criteria, you will need to make some changes so that it does.

Activity 5

 **ASSESSMENT POINT**

▷ Open your spreadsheet model and make any changes that you think are necessary.

Don't forget to save any changes.

Submit your amended spreadsheet model here. **SUBMIT**

ASSESS TO PROGRESS

Self assessment

 ASSESS

Wrapping it up

Activity 6

▷ As a class, discuss:
● why testing is necessary
● why testing leads to further improvements of a system.

Homework

To prepare for the next lesson about surveys, look for a questionnaire in a magazine or newspaper at home and write down:
● who it is aimed at
● what the point of the questions is
● how many questions there are
● how many questions are designed to be answered yes/no.

Unit 3.7

Question time

IN THIS LESSON

You will:

- Use your knowledge of global warming to decide on questions to use in a questionnaire

- Design a questionnaire to be used to survey opinions

CAPABILITY

- Decide on the questions to include in your questionnaire

- Identify the types of question to use to get the correct results

ASSESSMENT POINTS

	At level 4, you:	At level 5, you:	At level 6, you:
1	Choose appropriate closed questions for your survey to give you clear and simple answers	Choose both open and closed questions that are clear and easy to understand for all of your target audience	Design an easy to use questionnaire that makes good use of both open and closed questions that are clear and easy to understand for all of your target audience
2	Can design a questionnaire to collect pupils' opinions on global warming	Can design a questionnaire to collect pupils' opinions on global warming, making use of feedback to ensure the questionnaire works properly	Choose the best way to collect responses for your survey, making use of feedback to improve your completed questionnaire design

Getting started

Now that you have finished your model, the Global Warming Agency has asked you to create some leaflets or posters to advertise your model in school to encourage pupils, teachers and parents to use it.

The first thing you need to find out is what message would get people's attention. What is important to your audience? You are going to conduct a **survey** to find out the opinions of a specific group of people – the pupils, teachers and parents at your school – and to do this you will use a **questionnaire**.

Let's go

Activity 1

▶ Look at this example of a questionnaire. The questions that are being asked are a little confusing.

● What is wrong with the questions?

● How could they be improved?

WP

Types of question

You are probably asked lots of different questions every day. Your teacher may already have asked you a question in this lesson! What you need to understand is the type of questions that are appropriate for a questionnaire.

Here are two examples of types of question:

Closed questions – for example 'Do you feel OK?' – This question will most likely be answered with a simple yes or no.

Open questions – for example 'How are you feeling today?' – This question might be answered with all kinds of responses.

WP

Activity 2

Remember, the point of the questionnaire is to find out what about global warming is of most interest to your audience, e.g. animals dying, disease increasing, etc.

Here is a list of questions to ask. You must include the first three. In small groups, read through the list and decide:

- which questions to include
- which questions need to be changed so that they are more clear
- why closed rather than open questions might be appropriate for your questionnaire.

You can use the questionnaire you found for your last homework to help you.

Once you have decided which questions to include, share your group's ideas with the class and prepare your list of questions.

Choose the answers

You probably now have a sensible list of questions that you can ask other pupils. To make your questions useful, you need to choose the answers for your closed questions that will allow pupils to answer them sensibly.

Activity 3

▶ As a class, choose the answers that people can select. Discuss:
- what the choices should be
- how many responses there should be.

Write down the questions and answers you have all decided on.

Design your questionnaire

Your next step is to create the questionnaire that you are going to use. Because you need to make sure that your questionnaire is easy to use, this will be a draft design – you will need to test it to make sure that it is suited to its purpose!

Activity 4

ASSESSMENT POINT

With the list of questions your class has decided on, design a basic layout for your questionnaire on paper. You need to consider:
- how you will lay out the questions
- where people will put their answers.

Wrapping it up

Activity 5

▶ As a class, discuss:
- how certain types of question will influence the answer that a person might give
- to what extent you should guide people in their answers when creating a questionnaire
- the importance of the design of a questionnaire.

Homework

Take your completed questionnaire design home with you. Ask a pupil, a teacher or a parent to answer the questionnaire and ask them for their opinions.
- Do they understand your questions?
- Do you get the answers you were expecting?

Unit 3.8

Get creative

IN THIS LESSON

You will:

- Decide how to lay out your questionnaire
- Create your questionnaire using appropriate software

CAPABILITY

- Lay out a document for a specific purpose
- Choose the tools required
- Format a document

TECHNIQUES

You will learn or revisit the following techniques:

- Insert a table
- Format a table
- Add rows to a table
- Format text
- Create a numbered list
- Use bullets
- Insert a column into a table
- Use shapes

ASSESSMENT POINTS

	At level 4, you:	At level 5, you:	At level 6, you:
1	Choose the features you think will be necessary in your questionnaire	Choose the features you think will be necessary in your questionnaire, identifying and using the software tools that will help you do this	
2	Create and format a questionnaire to collect pupils' opinions on global warming	Create and format a questionnaire to collect pupils' opinions on global warming, making use of feedback to ensure the questionnaire works properly	

Getting started

Activity 1

For your last homework, you collected feedback on your paper design of what your questionnaire is going to look like.

▶ In pairs, discuss:

● suggestions you have received on your designs

● what you might change about your designs

Let's go

Features of a questionnaire

You have probably all decided on a similar **layout** for your questionnaires and on which features you have included, and some of you might have made a few changes based on the comments you have been given!

Making a questionnaire is not as easy as it may seem. You need to choose carefully the software you are going to use to make it.

Activity 2

ASSESSMENT POINT

▶ Look at these images of completed questionnaires. As a class, discuss:

● what the advantages of each are

● what the disadvantages of each are

● what features are useful

▶ With a partner, discuss:

● which program you will use to make your questionnaire

● what features the questionnaire might need to make it look professional.

Share your ideas with the rest of the class and choose the program that you think is most suitable.

IMAGE

IMAGE

Make it!

You will have now decided on the program that you are going to use to make the questionnaire. Before you start, think about:

- who you are aiming the questionnaire at
- how it will be filled in – will they fill it in without help?
- how you will make it easy to use.

Can I do this?

Insert a table

DEMO

Format a table

DEMO

Add rows to a table

DEMO

Format text

DEMO

Create a numbered list

DEMO

Use bullets

DEMO

Insert a column into a table

DEMO

Use shapes

DEMO

Activity 3

ASSESSMENT POINT

▷ Open the program you are going to use to make your questionnaire and start adding your questions and answers.

Save your completed survey with a sensible filename.

Check it!

Last lesson you collected feedback on your completed design to make sure your questionnaire was easy to understand and use. Now that you have completed the questionnaire it is a good idea to check it for errors in **formatting.**

Activity 4

ASSESSMENT POINT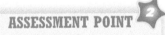

▷ Ask a partner to go through your questionnaire and look out for:
- spelling mistakes
- any confusion over the questions or answers.

Submit your questionnaire here **SUBMIT**

ASSESS TO PROGRESS

Self assessment

ASSESS

Wrapping it up

Activity 5

Your teacher will choose three finished questionnaires. As a class, discuss:

- whether the questionnaires are user friendly
- whether they are laid out appropriately
- whether they make good use of ICT tools.

Make any changes to your questionnaire that you think necessary and print out five copies of it.

Homework

Give your questionnaire printouts to other pupils, teachers or parents to complete. Alternatively, you could ask people to complete them by e-mail or using the school's collaborative tools, e.g. shared drive.

As this is going to be a class project, you all need to try and find a range of people to complete the questionnaire.

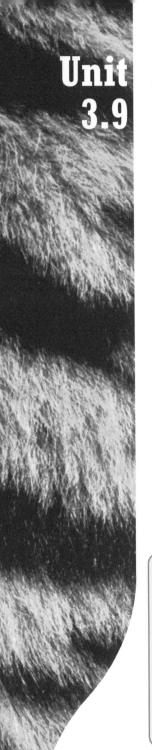

Unit 3.9

Analysing the results

IN THIS LESSON

You will:

- Enter the results of your survey
- Find out the information you need from the survey

CAPABILITY

- Enter data
- Put data into a database
- Search for information

TECHNIQUES

You will learn or revisit the following techniques:

- Create a table using database software
- Add validation to a database
- Add records to a database
- Create a query in a database

ASSESSMENT POINTS

	At level 4, you:	At level 5, you:	At level 6, you:
1	Understand that some of the data collected in your survey may not be useful and cannot be entered into your system	Can create a simple database structure and import the results of your survey into it	Can create a simple database structure and import the results of your survey into it, completing a simple check to ensure that the data has been imported
2	Create some simple queries using AND/OR to find useful results from your database of survey results	Create some queries using AND/OR/NOT to find information from your database of results, doing further searches if you don't find what you are looking for	Understand the way that data is stored in your database and use this knowledge to create more complex queries to find useful results from your survey

Getting started

Activity 1

▶ Take a look at the information or **data** on the worksheet and answer the questions.

WP

Let's go

Storing your results

Now you have completed your survey, your class will probably have quite a large number of responses to deal with. You need to analyse the data in order to find out how interested people are in different areas of global warming. It would take a long time to do this by hand. And if this were a bigger project, that might be hundreds or even thousands of people! Using a computer to do this allows you to analyse your findings quickly and easily.

You may also find that some of the responses are not **plausible** – some people may have entered their answers incorrectly. Using a computer to collect data means you can reject these responses.

Now it is time to enter your results. You will need to create a database table to store the responses to your questions.

Each question you have asked needs to be stored in a different **field**. Each person's answers will make up their individual **record** and all of the responses together are known as the database **file**.

Activity 2

▶ Open up the software you are going to use for this task and create a table to store the responses to your questionnaire. You will need to choose the correct data type for each response. Use the 'Can I do this?' activity to learn how to create your table.

Can I do this?

Create a table using database software

 DEMO

Add validation to a database

DEMO

Entering your results

Now you have created your database table, you will need to add the responses that you have collected. As you have only collected 5 responses yourself, you will need to add some records from some of your classmates. To have an appropriate list to search, you should aim to add the records from 5 of your classmates so that you have approximately 20 - 25 records in your database.

Activity 3

▶ Open up your database table and add the records from your collected questionnaires. Use the 'Can I do this?' activity to show you how to add the responses to your database.

What to analyse?

Before you start to do any kind of analysis, it is a good idea to decide what you are going to look for.

Can I do this?

Add records to a database

DEMO

Activity 4

ASSESSMENT POINT

▶ As a class, discuss:
● what you will be using the results for
● what the important data is
● what you will need to look for.

Do you have a query?

You have now decided what the important data is that you need to identify. Now you need to investigate what you have found as a result of your survey.

To do this you are going to **query** the database. A query is simply a question – a bit like asking how many girls and boys are in your ICT class.

Imagine that when you wanted to add friends to your instant messenger account you had to find them from a list of all the users on instant messenger! There are already millions of people who have these accounts in the UK so it would probably take you a very long time indeed. A database can do this for us in seconds.

Activity 5

Extend

ASSESSMENT POINT

If you haven't already opened the database software, do so now and use queries to find which problems with global warming are most important to your target audience of pupils, teachers and parents. Save each query that you have made with an appropriate filename.

Can I do this?

Create a query in a database

DEMO

Wrapping it up

Activity 6

▶ As a class, discuss:

⬤ why databases are useful for storing and searching for information.

You have now found out which areas of the environment pupils, parents and teachers are most interested in. This will help you to create your poster or leaflet.

Homework

In the next lesson you will create a report for the GWA. Make a list of 3 features you think a good report should contain.

Unit 3.10

Present your findings

IN THIS LESSON

You will:

- Decide how to present your findings
- Choose the information to include
- Consider how to make a document fit for purpose

CAPABILITY

- Consider how the findings of your survey should be presented
- Identify the important information to include
- Learn how to make a report
- Learn how to present your findings

TECHNIQUES

You will learn or revisit the following techniques:

- Create a report using database software
- Format a report
- Insert an image into a report
- Insert a chart into a report

ASSESSMENT POINTS

	At level 4, you:	At level 5, you:	At level 6, you:
1	Present the results of your queries as a report, ensuring that the report gives a clear explanation of what you have found		
2		Present the results of your queries in a report	Present the results of your queries in a report, formatting the report to be appropriate for the purpose
3	Describe an example of an electronic database that you have used or seen in use	Describe how databases can be useful, using an example of a database you have used or seen in use	Describe the problems of storing data on an electronic database and how databases can be useful, using an example you have used or seen in use

Getting started

In the last lesson you found out what areas of the environment were of most interest to pupils, parents and teachers. This will help you to create the messages for your poster or leaflet. But first the Global Warming Agency (GWA) wants you to compare your results with results from a national survey and create a **report** to show them what you have found out from your questionnaire.

Using a large dataset

Last lesson you queried the results you found from your questionnaire. Now you need to compare them with the results from a national survey.

Activity 1

▶ Open this dataset and query the results using similar queries to those you used last lesson on your own data. Record the results.

DB

Let's go

Create a report

Activity 2

Do you remember how to create a report and what features are important? Discuss the features you chose for homework.
Look at this example. Here a pupil has presented the findings of a survey of how many children like school dinners. What is wrong with this report? As a class, discuss the report.

WP

How to present your findings

You will have noted from the last activity that the pupil had not really presented his or her findings very well. The way you show what you found is as important as the investigation itself.

Your report needs to detail:

- the category of person (pupil, teacher or parent)
- what areas of global warming are of most interest to them
- how these compare with the national figures.

Activity 3

- ▶ In small groups, discuss:
- ● what information you will include in each report – e.g. is there any information that might not be useful?
- ● should you include graphs?
- ● how the reports should be presented.

Can I do this?

Create a report using database software

DEMO ◯

Format a report

DEMO ◯

Insert an image into a report

DEMO ◯

Insert a chart into a report

DEMO ◯

Activity 4

ASSESSMENT POINTS

It is now time to create the report that you are going to use to present your findings.

- ▶ Remind yourself of the techniques you will need to use for making your report.
- ▶ Save your report using an appropriate filename.

Fit for purpose

You are expected to present these completed reports to the GWA, so they must look **fit for purpose**. You may need to modify the reports so that they look professional.

Activity 5

- ▶ With a partner, have a look at each other's reports and discuss:
- ● whether the completed reports look good enough to submit
- ● whether there are any errors that need to be fixed.

IMAGE

Make your changes
Now you have evaluated your reports, you need to make any changes that you think are necessary to make them look good.

Activity 6 Extend

▷ Open your first report and make whatever changes you think are necessary.

▷ Remind yourself of the techniques you will need to use for editing your report.

▷ Amend each of your reports until they are fit for purpose.

Submit your completed report here **SUBMIT**

Wrapping it up

Activity 7

ASSESSMENT POINT

▷ As a class, discuss:
● where databases are used
● what impact databases have upon our lives
● the problems related to using databases and storing data on a computer.

ASSESS TO PROGRESS

Self assessment   ASSESS

Peer assessment
Ask a partner to complete the peer assessment checklist in your profile.

Homework

In the next lesson, you will be creating your poster.

Choose one group of your audience, i.e. pupils, teachers or parents. Look at the areas of global warming they said they were most worried about. Think about how you will use this information to create a headline message for your poster or leaflet. For example, if they said 'illness', your headline could be 'Malaria will be here soon – unless you help stop it!' Remember, you are trying to get the attention of your audience.

You could look at this website for poster ideas.

WWW

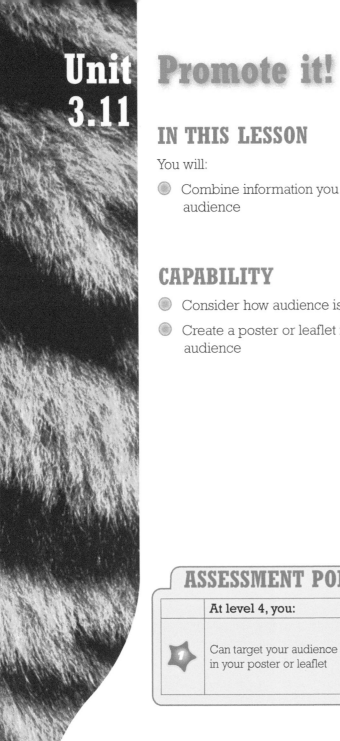

Unit 3.11

Promote it!

IN THIS LESSON

You will:

- Combine information you have found to create a poster or leaflet for a specific audience

CAPABILITY

- Consider how audience is targeted
- Create a poster or leaflet for a specific audience

TECHNIQUES

You will learn or revisit the following techniques:

- Use a text box
- Use WordArt
- Format text
- Use bullets
- Insert an image
- Print preview
- Save your work

ASSESSMENT POINTS

	At level 4, you:	At level 5, you:	At level 6, you:
	Can target your audience in your poster or leaflet	Create a poster or leaflet that shows you understand your audience and the purpose of the poster or leaflet	Create a poster or leaflet that shows a clear understanding of your audience and the purpose of the poster or leaflet, making good use of ICT tools

Getting started

Now you have all the information you need, you can create your poster or leaflet. Remember that there are many areas to think about when planning a poster or leaflet. Important factors are:

- audience
- purpose
- message
- design.

Activity 1

▷ Take a look at these examples of a poster. As a class, discuss the factors above.

Now discuss these factors for your own poster or leaflet.

IMAGE

IMAGE

Let's go

How do you target your audience?

You have several audiences who you want to use your calculator model: pupils, parents and teachers. You have probably already found through your questionnaire that they have different interests. To make your poster or leaflet most effective, you should **target** one of these groups so that you can really make your message grab their attention.

Activity 2

As a class, discuss what you wrote down at the start of the lesson – how will you target your audience for this poster or leaflet? What will your message be?

Is it fit for purpose?

Once you know your audience, you need to decide what this poster or leaflet is going to do – you should already know that it is to try to encourage people to use your model.

But how will you make sure that the poster or leaflet gets the message across?

Activity 3

▶ As a class, discuss:

● what images you should put into the poster or leaflet and where you might find them (remember – you may not be able to use everything on the Internet because of copyright)

● appropriate headlines

● what information you should include

● how you will persuade people to use your model

● when and where people will be able to access your model, e.g. by e-mail, on a website, at school?

Can I do this?

Use a text box

DEMO ○

Use WordArt

DEMO ○

Format text

DEMO ○

Use bullets

DEMO ○

Insert an image

DEMO ○

Print preview

DEMO ○

Save your work

DEMO ○

Create your poster/leaflet

Your challenge is to create the poster or leaflet to make pupils aware of your survey.

Activity 4

ASSESSMENT POINT ⭐

▶ Open your desktop publishing software and make a simple poster or leaflet to **publicise** your model. You should include:

● a suitable image

● a fact about global warming

● why pupils should use your calculator model, i.e. how it can help them

● how and when they can access the calculator model.

Save your poster or leaflet in an appropriate place.

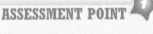

Submit your completed poster or leaflet here **SUBMIT** ○

ASSESS TO PROGRESS

Self assessment

ASSESS ○

Wrapping it up

Activity 5

▶ As a class, look at two or three examples of your completed posters or leaflets and discuss:

● how the audience has been targeted

● whether the posters are suitable for purpose.

Homework

In the next lesson you will begin to create a simulation of an electronic card tracking system for your school.

ICT tools have been used in lots of different ways to track people's movements. For homework write down:

◉ A list of ways in which ICT tools are used to trace people's movements.

◉ Why tracking using ICT might be a good thing.

◉ Any disadvantages to tracking you can think of.

Unit challenge: An e-card system for your school

Your tasks in this unit

Technology can help keep schools safe places to be by tracking users. It can help check that people entering school are supposed to be there, it can keep pupils out of dangerous places, it can protect delicate equipment and it can even help to stop pupils losing their money!

Your head teacher has decided that your school ought to have an electronic card system to help solve two main problems:

● Queues in the school canteen are always too long. People forget to bring money, or don't have the right amount.

● Locked doors to rooms which have dangerous or expensive equipment. This is annoying for teachers because they have to carry lots of keys.

Over the next eight lessons you will:

1 Discuss how the card could be used in your school

2 Create a simulation of a card system

3 Test your simulation

Do we really need tracking?

Some schools already use tracking systems. Look at these links and think about these questions:

- What are the benefits for pupils?
- What are the benefits for staff?
- Can you think of any disadvantages?

WWW

WWW

Is it good or bad?

"My card doesn't let me buy more than three bars of chocolate per week. That's not fair – it's none of its business!"

Kobe, Leicester

"Our pupil cards track which buses we ride on; I feel safe knowing people know where I am going."

Liam, Yorkshire

"My school is in the middle of a city and sometimes there are weird people around. Our security system helps keep the school safe."

Michaela, Birmingham

"I love my student card, because I can buy things in the local shops too."

Hardeep, Aberdeen

"I lost my card and now the school thinks I bunked off."

Emma, Somerset

"I don't want a card. What if it got stolen? – someone might be able to use it or to find things out about me."

Shannon, Essex

"I can never remember my PIN so I've told my best friend. She always remembers – and she'd never tell anyone."

Laetitia, London

How much tracking is right?

ICT tools are used in lots of different ways to track people's movements. These websites show you a few examples. Can you think of any more?

WWW

WWW

Unit 4.1 Putting things in order

IN THIS LESSON

You will:

- Think about what an electronic card system for the school needs to be able to do
- Find out about how cards work in principle
- Try out a simulation of a card system

CAPABILITY

- Consider how electronic cards are used all around us
- Identify the key areas of the problem
- Analyse other people's work
- Start to plan your own card

ASSESSMENT POINTS

	At level 4, you:	At level 5, you:	
1	Know that sets of instructions need to be planned before execution	Know that sequencing instructions is the foundation to a wide range of ICT applications	

Getting started...

Your head teacher has decided that your school ought to have an **electronic card system** to help solve two problems:

- Queues in the school canteen are always too long.
- Doors to rooms which have dangerous or expensive equipment sometimes have to be locked.

Your head teacher says that the card must help solve these problems, but would like to know what other problems the card might be able to solve. Who better to investigate these possibilities than the ICT class?

What do electronic cards do?

You have probably already used an electronic card or **identity system** yourself. There are lots of different types, and they all do different things. The things they do are called **functions**.

Activity 1

▶ Look at this video. As a class, write a list of types of identity systems shown and what they do.

VIDEO

Let's go

You are going to concentrate on electronic card (or e-card) systems.

Activity 2

▶ As a class:
- open the electronic card system ideas generator
- discuss and write down all the different electronic cards you can think of and what their functions are
- save a copy of your work with an appropriate filename in your user area.

WP

If you're stuck, have a look at the ideas in the unit introduction. These may help you to come up with more ideas of your own.

What could the school card system do?

Now think about your school card system. Your head teacher wants to make the canteen and room access as efficient as possible.

Activity 3

- With a partner, discuss and write down what you think the card system ought to be able to do to help the canteen and room access to be more efficient.
- Now discuss what other functions the card could have in other areas of the school.
- Discuss your points as a class and record your ideas on the electronic card system planning sheet.

Now submit your planning sheet here. **SUBMIT**

Creating an electronic card system takes a lot of work. There isn't much point in creating it, only to find it doesn't work. So you are going to create a **simulation** of a card system.

The simulation for your system has already been started. You will improve it.

What does the e-card system do at the moment?

Activity 4

As a class, open the e-card simulation spreadsheet and save a copy to your user area, using a sensible filename. Explore how this simulation works, using the tabs at the bottom of the sheet to help you navigate. Answer the questions in the electronic card simulation evaluation sheet, and save a copy in your user area.

Welcome to the e-card simulation

1. Enter your name
2. Enter your PIN and press 'return'
3. Click the 'Enter' button

User 1	Enter Pin

Enter

Activity 5

Compare the e-card simulation you looked at in Activity 4 with the planning sheet you completed in Activity 3.

On your evaluation sheet, write down what improvements could be made to the simulation spreadsheet.

Now submit your evaluation sheet here. **SUBMIT**

Wrapping it up

Activity 6

As a class discuss your ideas for improvements to the system.
In the following lessons you will make some of these improvements.

Homework

Your head teacher wants the card to be secure, using a **PIN (Personal Identification Number)**. This is used like a password to show that you really are who you say you are.

For homework, write down step-by-step instructions for checking someone's PIN. For example, the first three steps might be:

1. Insert card
2. Enter name
3. Check if name is on system

Sequencing and flow charts

IN THIS LESSON

You will:

- Create flow charts for your simulation
- Understand the importance of making instructions accurate and precise

CAPABILITY

- Understand what sequencing is
- Learn how flow charts represent a sequence of events
- Understand why it is important to make your instructions accurate and precise

TECHNIQUES

You will learn or revisit the following techniques:

- Create a flow chart
- Format a flow chart

ASSESSMENT POINTS

	At level 4, you:	At level 5, you:	At level 6, you:
1	Can plan sets of instructions before creating your e-card		
2			Understand that complex information systems can be represented in a diagrammatical form in order to support their development
3		Can use precise and accurate language when creating instructions	

Getting started...

Activity 1

▶ Look again at the video of people using different electronic systems.

- What order did they do things in? Complete these drag and drop activities.

- What would happen if you did things in the wrong order?

VIDEO

D+D

D+D

Let's go

Sequencing

Almost all systems use **sequencing**, or putting instructions in the correct order.

If you did the Gaming challenge in ActiveBook 1, you will have met the idea of sequencing before. Things happened in an order: for example, first the object hit a wall, then it made a noise and bounced.

Activity 2   Support

 ASSESSMENT POINT ⭐ 1

Remember, sequencing is about putting instructions in the right order.

▶ As a class, discuss the order of the step-by-step instructions you created for homework.

▶ Now discuss the order of the steps you wrote down. Does it matter what order they appear in?

Introducing flow charts

Flow charts are diagrams that help us to plan and show what order instructions should happen in, i.e. they show us the sequence of events.

Flow charts use special symbols which make it clear what is happening.

Try it out with the PIN system you created for homework.

The flow chart for this will look something like this diagram. The different shapes show what each step is about.

If the PIN is correct, it opens the menu screen.

If the PIN is not correct, it allows the user to try again.

WP

Can I do this?

Create a flow chart
DEMO ◯

Format a flow chart
DEMO ◯

Activity 3

ASSESSMENT POINT 2

With a partner, write out a flow chart for the step-by-step instructions you created for homework for entering a PIN.

Activity 4   Extend

As you have seen from the e-card simulation spreadsheet, you are allowed to access different rooms. The card checks whether you are allowed to enter the room or not.

▶ Look at the Enter rooms sheet again. Try changing the username on the Welcome sheet and see if that makes a difference.

▶ With your partner, write out the flow chart for this.

What do you mean?

When you write instructions it is very important to make them accurate. Sometimes you can give an instruction meaning one thing, but someone else will think you mean something else. It can also be very easy to miss an obvious step.

This is particularly important when writing instructions for computers. Computers cannot think about the instructions to try to work out what you meant. They just do *exactly* what you have told them.

Activity 5

ASSESSMENT POINT 3

WP ◯

▶ Take a look at these instructions for making a cup of tea. Do they make sense?

▶ Now look at this video of someone following the instructions.

  ● Which instructions were unclear? Why?

VIDEO ◯

Many of the tea-making instructions were **ambiguous**. People can usually **interpret** these to understand what is meant. Computers cannot do this. Instructions must be **precise** and clear.

Activity 6 Extend

ASSESSMENT POINT

Swap your PIN and door opening flow charts with another pair and check each other's work. Are the instructions precise? Is anything ambiguous or missing?

Now submit your flow chart here. **SUBMIT**

Wrapping it up

Activity 7

ASSESS TO PROGRESS

Self assessment

Peer assessment

ASSESS

▶ As a class:
  ● discuss some of your flow charts
  ● discuss any problems you had
  ● discuss how the problems might be solved.

Homework

Look at the flow chart you created in Activity 3 for entering a PIN. Write down the **decisions** which need to be made.

Unit 4.3

Security

IN THIS LESSON

You will:

- Find out why security is important for your e-card
- Write a formula which checks whether the user's PIN is correct

CAPABILITY

- Understand why security is important
- Use decisions and the IF function

TECHNIQUES

You will learn or revisit the following techniques:

- Use the IF function

ASSESSMENT POINTS

	At level 4, you:	At level 5, you:	
1	Show that a set of instructions can be rationalised by repeating sections	Can use precise and accurate language when creating instructions	

Getting started...

Activity 1

▶ As a class, discuss why security is important for your e-card. Now discuss any disadvantages to having this security.

Let's go

Security

Most security checks use a password or Personal Identity Number (PIN) that only the owner knows. That is why it is important never to share this information with anyone. For your card system, you are going to use a PIN.

Decisions and the IF function

In a flow chart, decisions often include a question, then different outcomes according to whether the answer is yes or no.

This is very similar to IF functions. In the example you saw in Unit 3, the statement was:

'If it is raining, I will take an umbrella, otherwise I won't.'

In a flow chart, this becomes

To work out what the IF function will be, you can first write it in words:

If	If it is raining
Then	I will take an umbrella
Else	I won't take an umbrella

Activity 2

▶ As a class, discuss:
- the decisions you found from your flow chart for homework
- how you could represent these as IF statements, e.g. IF PIN is correct, then ..., otherwise ...

Using the IF function

IF statements in Excel use as few words as possible!

An IF formula looks like this,

IF [a condition is true], [then ....], [else ....]

You need to create a formula to work out whether the PIN is correct or not.

The user will enter their PIN on the Welcome sheet of the e-card simulation spreadsheet.

The Data sheet works out what the user's PIN should be.

You can display one message for a correct PIN and another for an incorrect PIN.

Activity 3 Extend

ASSESSMENT POINTS

▶ Write a formula on a cell on the Menu sheet to work out whether or not the PIN is correct and display one message for a correct PIN and another for an incorrect PIN.

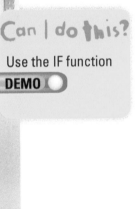

Can I do this?

Use the IF function

DEMO

Activity 4

▶ Team up with a friend and test each other's spreadsheet. Make any necessary changes.

Don't worry that it currently shows an error message before the user has a chance to enter their PIN, you will improve this later.

More decisions

Decisions occur a lot in sequences, often when the user enters some information. You will be adding more decisions in other parts of your spreadsheet.

Activity 5

▷ Take a look at the Menu sheet in your e-card simulation spreadsheet. With a partner, write down any decisions which might use an IF function.

Wrapping it up

Activity 6

▷ As a class, discuss:
- the importance of security to the system
- how IF functions can represent decisions in a flow chart
- any problems you have found.

Homework

The school has conducted a survey of what pupils think about the card simulation so far. There were a lot of comments about the snack machine part of the card (on the Menu sheet):

- On the snack machine, I want to know if I have enough money on my card to afford my snacks.
- We need to make sure we eat healthily. The card should stop you eating more than two bars of chocolate.
- We need to eat more healthily, but it is not up to a machine to decide what we buy. If someone buys more than two bars of chocolate, the machine should give them a message to remind them that too much chocolate is bad for you.

Choose one of these viewpoints. On this sheet, write down the sequence of events that will need to happen and create a flow chart.

Buying snacks

IN THIS LESSON

You will:

- Look at the advantages and disadvantages of the snack machine function of the card
- Create messages to be displayed to the user if they can't afford their snacks
- Insert messages if the user purchases too much chocolate

CAPABILITY

- Plan your sequences using flow charts
- Write accurate formulae
- Give appropriate feedback to the user
- Test your formulae to ensure they are working correctly

TECHNIQUES

You will learn or revisit the following techniques:

- Use the IF function
- Use a Remote IF
- Use a Nested IF
- Name a cell

ASSESSMENT POINTS

	At level 4, you:	At level 5, you:	
1	Can plan sets of instructions before creating your e-card		
2		Can use precise and accurate language when creating instructions	

Getting started...

Activity 1

▶ As a class, discuss the viewpoints of the pupils you looked at for homework. What are the advantages and disadvantages of having the snack machine facility on the electronic card?

Let's go

Activity 2

ASSESSMENT POINTS **1** **2**

For homework, you created flow charts for new functions in the simulation. Discuss these as a class and share them so that everyone can see a copy of a flow chart for each viewpoint.

You are going to use these flow charts to help you create solutions to the views given in the survey. These will build on your knowledge of IF statements.

Can you afford it?

How would the card 'know' if you had enough money on your card to be able to afford to make your purchase?

Can I do this?

Use the IF function

DEMO

Activity 3

In cell E12 on the Menu sheet in your e-card simulation spreadsheet, change the formula so that it will check whether the user can afford the purchase.

IF	Then	Else
They can't afford it	Display a message to tell them	Display the sum of their purchase

Use what you have learnt so far in terms of the IF function and the flow chart you created for homework.

Can I do this?

Use a Remote IF

DEMO

Giving further useful feedback

Pupils wish to have more information about healthier options. You can display more information to the user, but in a different cell. This can be a useful way of providing information without cluttering up the same part of the screen. It is sometimes called a 'Remote IF'.

Activity 4   Extend

▶ Add a formula so that, as well as being warned about buying too many chocolate bars, the user is given the URL of a healthy eating website below the total spent column.

Healthy eating

The pupils at your school want to eat more healthily. One way that the card system can help is by warning people when they are about to purchase too many chocolate bars. To make it neat, you can display this in the same cell as the formula from Activity 3.

In words, the IF statement might look like this.

IF	Then	Else			
They can't afford it	Display a message to tell them	IF	Then	Else	
		They have too many chocolate bars	display a message to tell them	display the sum of their purchases	

As you can see, one IF statement is nested inside the other. This is known as a 'Nested IF'. You will need to create a formula for this.

Activity 5

▷ Go back to the formula you created in Activity 3 and insert a message depending on how many chocolate bars were purchased, using a 'Nested IF' approach. You should draft the sequence on paper before entering a formula in the spreadsheet, using and amending your flow chart to help you.

▷ Look at the important cells used in Activity 5. Name any that aren't already named and amend your formulae to use these named ranges.

Can I do this?
Use a Nested IF
◖ **DEMO**

Can I do this?
Name a cell
◖ **DEMO**

Activity 6

▷ Change places with a friend, and test each other's spreadsheet. Check that you can't buy anything if you don't have enough money on your card, and that you're given useful information if you try to buy too many chocolate bars.

● Make any amendments necessary.

Submit your spreadsheet here. **SUBMIT**

ASSESS TO PROGRESS
Self assessment
Peer assessment
◖ **ASSESS**

Wrapping it up

Activity 7

As a class discuss the difference between IF, Remote IF and Nested IF.

Homework

Write a summary of what you use IF, Remote IF and Nested IF for.

Unit 4.5

Making it work better

IN THIS LESSON

You will:

- Start to write macro code

CAPABILITY

- Write accurate instructions
- Write your instructions efficiently using macros
- Test your sequences to ensure they are working accurately

TECHNIQUES

You will learn or revisit the following techniques:

- Open Visual Basic Editor
- Introduction to Visual Basic Editor
- Create a sub procedure
- Create a message box
- Run a macro
- Add sound
- Debug your code
- Create a repeating code

ASSESSMENT POINTS

	At level 4, you:	At level 5, you:	At level 6, you:
1		Can test and refine sequences of instructions in order to achieve specific outcomes	Can break down a problem into smaller sections that can be represented by sub-procedures
2			Show how the efficient structuring of instructions increases flexibility and makes testing easier

Getting started...

If you look at the Welcome sheet on your e-card simulation spreadsheet, you'll see that as soon as you select a user, you get an error message. In real life, you actually press a button to confirm you have finished. To do that you need to use a **macro** or **procedure**. This is a sequence of steps that the computer will perform automatically.

Activity 1

▶ Look at this spreadsheet. It contains some different macros. Click on the buttons and write a list of what these macros are doing.

Let's go

What can macros do?

Macros can allow you to add more functions to your system. For example, you can give messages to the user when they press a button. This lesson you are going to create some messages.

Macros use language called Visual Basic for Applications (VBA). It is a bit like Logo, which you may have used at primary school. It is a programming language that gives instructions to computers in the form of code.

When you write macros, you group a set of instructions into a step called a **sub procedure**.

Activity 2

ASSESSMENT POINT **1**

Now you can start programming!

▶ Open your e-card simulation spreadsheet and open Visual Basic Editor.

▶ Look at the 'Can I do this?' activities

   ● Create a new sub procedure called 'Welcome_msg'.

   ● Write code for a message box with the text 'Welcome'.

   ● Run your macro to test it works.

Can I do this?

Open Visual Basic Editor

◖ DEMO

Introduction to Visual Basic Editor

◖ DEMO

Create a sub procedure

◖ DEMO

Create a message box

◖ DEMO

Run a macro

◖ DEMO

Activity 3

ASSESSMENT POINT

You need a message to appear when people get their PIN wrong, reminding them that they need to select their username, enter their PIN, press Return and then click 'Enter'.

Create a new sub procedure for this message called 'Pin_ instructions' and run it to check it works.

Audio confirmation

Have you noticed that systems often have audio confirmation or warning when they need you to do something? When users have finished withdrawing cash from an ATM, it will beep at them to remind them to take their card. If you try to close a word-processing document without saving, it will beep to warn you and ask if you want to save.

You are going to create one for your simulation.

Activity 4

ASSESSMENT POINTS

- Create a new procedure called 'Beeps'.
- Make it beep three times.
- Run your procedure to test it.

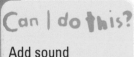

Can I do this?

Add sound

DEMO

If, when you run your macro, you get an error message the Visual Basic Editor will highlight your code so that you can correct it. Have a look at this 'Can I do this?' demonstration.

Can I do this?

Debug your code

DEMO

Repeating code

Your Beeps macro contains the same code three times. You can write code that is more efficient by repeating code. If you have used Logo before, you may be familiar with the command REPEAT. Macros also allow you to repeat code, but with a different command.

Can I do this?

Create repeating code

Activity 5

ASSESSMENT POINTS **1** **2**

Change your Beeps macro to use a repeating code.

Wrapping it up

Activity 6

▶ As a class, discuss:
- why macros are useful
- any problems you had writing your macro code.

Homework

Write a flow chart for each step of the Beeps macro you have just written. Think about how you could improve it.

Check the PIN

IN THIS LESSON

You will:

● Write the first part of the code that checks the user's PIN

CAPABILITY

● Write accurate instructions

● Write your instructions efficiently using macros

● Test your sequences to ensure they are working accurately

TECHNIQUES

You will learn or revisit the following techniques:

● Name a cell

● Use the IF function within a macro

● Run a macro

● Assign a macro

ASSESSMENT POINTS

	At level 5, you:	At level 6, you:	
1	Can test and refine sequences of instructions in order to achieve specific outcomes	Can break down a problem into smaller sections that can be represented by sub procedures	
2		Show how the efficient structuring of instructions increases flexibility and makes testing easier	

Getting started...

You are going to improve the PIN system.

Activity 1

First look at this sequence for the new PIN system. Put the steps in the right order.

Let's go

D+D

Repeating actions

You can see from Activity 1 that a large part of the flow chart could be repeated several times. It also introduced a 'submit' button so the system can tell when the user is finished. You can't do this with an IF statement. You need to use a mini-program called a macro, which can do lots of things much faster than a formula.

You can create a macro which stores several tasks. When you run the macro, it makes these tasks happen automatically.

Look at the flow chart you created in Activity 1. The macro would start to run at 'submit'. So the first stage is 'Is PIN correct?'.

In Unit 4.3 you used the IF statement:

If
[Then]
[Else]

Macros use a very similar statement:

If
Then
Else
End If

The 'End If' just tells the code that the IF statement has finished.

So, as before, you just need to check that the PIN the user has entered = the correct PIN. This time you need to use the name of the cell.

Activity 2

Can I do this?

Name a cell

DEMO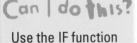

As a class:
● Click on the cell where the user enters their PIN. The cell has been named. What is its name?
● Go to the Data sheet and click on the cell next to 'Correct PIN'. This has also been named. What is its name?

It isn't quite enough to give the name of the cell. You need the macro to look at the **value** of the cell. For example:

```
Range(cell reference).value
```

'.value' is called the 'property' which looks at the content of the cell. Another example of a property is '.select' which would select the cell.

In this case, therefore, you will need to use `range("cardnumber").value` and `range("mynumber").value`.

Activity 3

Can I do this?

Use the IF function within a macro

DEMO

You should now be able to start your macro:
● Create a new macro called 'check_pin'
● Write the line of code starting 'IF...'.

If the PIN is correct, you need to give a welcome message. Remember, the code for displaying a message is `Msgbox "message"`.

If the PIN is incorrect, you need to give a message that says the PIN is incorrect.

Activity 4

▶ Write the next two lines of code.
● Then add 'End If' at the end to show that you have finished the IF statement.

Activity 5

- Finish your code.
- Discuss your code with a partner to check it is right.
- Run it to test it.

Can I do this?

Run a macro

DEMO

Running a macro from a button
You need to add a button so the user can run your macro from the spreadsheet. You will **assign** a macro to the 'Enter' button.

Activity 6

▷ Open your e-card simulation spreadsheet and assign a macro to the 'Enter' button.

Can I do this?

Assign a macro

DEMO

Wrapping it up

Activity 7

You have made a good start with your macro, which you will build on next lesson.

▷ As a class, look at this spreadsheet. What happens when you click on the 'check chocolate' button?

▷ Look at the code and write down the IF statement for the code. (Hint – it is like a Nested IF.)

Homework

Think about which sub procedures might happen more than once. For example, a 'Thank you' message might appear on several screens.

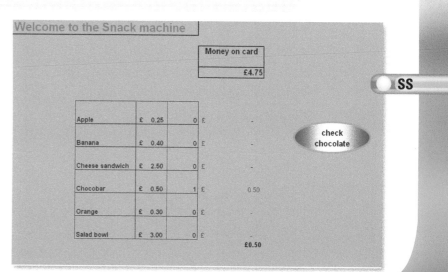

SS

Unit 4.7 — Cracking the code

IN THIS LESSON

You will:

- Identify procedures which are used more than once
- Write and use procedures to make your code efficient

CAPABILITY

- Write accurate instructions
- Write your instructions efficiently using macros
- Automate frequently used processes by constructing sub procedures
- Use software tools to automate tasks
- Test your sequences to ensure they are working accurately
- Make systems more efficient through automation

TECHNIQUES

You will learn or revisit the following techniques:

- Call a sub procedure
- Select a sheet
- Use macro recorder
- Create a repeating code

ASSESSMENT POINTS

	At level 4, you:	At level 5, you:	At level 6, you:
1	Can rationalise a set of instructions by repeating sections	Can use precise and accurate language when creating instructions	Understand how the efficient structuring of instructions increases flexibility and makes testing easier
2		Can test and refine sequences of instructions in order to achieve specific outcomes	Can break down a problem into smaller sections that can be represented by sub procedures

Getting started...

In any system, the same procedure may happen more than once. For example, the message 'Welcome' might appear on the Welcome sheet, the Menu sheet and the Enter rooms sheet.

Activity 1

▶ As a class, discuss other procedures which might happen more than once.

Let's go

Efficient code

Whilst it is possible to add code for each of these sections, it is a bit boring and takes a long time. It would be easier if you could just write the code once. Well, you can!

Once you have written it, you can simply 'call' a sub procedure by its name as part of another sub procedure and it will run.

We can use this to add some warning beeps to the end of your PIN macro.

Activity 2

ASSESSMENT POINT

▶ Open the 'check_pin' macro you wrote in the last lesson.
  ● Before **'End If'**, add Beeps (remember this was the sub procedure you wrote in Unit 4.5).
  ● Run your code.

Can I do this?

Call a sub procedure

DEMO

Activity 3

ASSESSMENT POINT

The user might need to be reminded what to do. Change your code to display the PIN instructions if they get it wrong. (Remember, you created a sub in Unit 4.5 called 'Pin_instructions' which does this.)

Automatic display

It would be useful to display these instructions when the user first opens the e-card simulation. You can do this by calling the macro 'sub auto_open'. This 'tells' the macro to run automatically when the file is opened.

Can I do this?

Select a sheet

DEMO

Activity 4   Support

▶ Create a sub 'auto_open' which:

- – selects the 'Welcome' sheet
- – displays the PIN instructions in a message box.

Automatic code!

So far you have written all the code yourself. But sometimes you can use a tool to help you called **macro recorder**. This 'records' actions you do and writes down the code for these actions in a macro, e.g. you can make text flash different colours.

Activity 5

ASSESSMENT POINTS

Can I do this?

Use macro recorder

DEMO

Can I do this?

Create a repeating code

DEMO

- On the Welcome sheet, select the cell where users enter their PIN.
- Using macro recorder, record a macro called 'Pin_flash'.
- Record changing the background to red and back to white.
- Edit this macro to add a 'wait' of 1 second between flashes.
- Also add a beep.
- Also add a repeat so it flashes red and beeps 3 times.
- Save your file.
- Go to your 'check_pin' sub procedure and change the code to call Pin_flash instead of Beeps when the user gets the PIN wrong.
- Run your code to test it.

Wrapping it up

Activity 6

Discuss the advantages and disadvantages of automatic ways of writing or using code (macro recorder, 'calling' frequently used sub procedures, automatically displaying when a file is opened).

Homework

It is important to test your simulation. You have tested it as you work, but you need to think about the following questions:

- Does it work?
- Is it easy to use?
- How could I make it better?

Start testing

IN THIS LESSON

You will:

- Create a test plan for your simulation
- Test your simulation
- Write a short report

CAPABILITY

- Test and refine instructions to make sure they are fit for purpose
- Structure and sequence information to meet the purpose
- Refine the presentation of information to meet the purpose

ASSESSMENT POINTS

	At level 5, you:	At level 6, you:	
1	Can test and refine sequences of instructions in order to achieve specific outcomes	Can break down a problem into smaller sections that can be represented by sub procedures	
2	Can structure and sequence information to meet audience needs		
3	Can use a range of ICT tools efficiently to refine the presentation of information for a specific purpose		
4		Understand and demonstrate how to apply your learning in future work	

Getting started...

It is important to test your simulation to make sure it meets your success criteria.

Activity 1

▶ As a class, discuss what needs to be tested. Think about the notes you made for homework to help you.

Let's go

In order to test your simulation effectively, you need a test plan so testers know exactly what they are going to test.

Activity 2

▶ Using your answers to Activity 1, and the test plan you created in Unit 3 (page 91), create a test plan for your testing.

Activity 3

ASSESSMENT POINTS

▶ Now your test plan is complete, divide into groups of three.
  ● First test your own simulation and record your findings on your test plan.
  ● Then, each person should test both of the other pupils' simulations and record them on the relevant test plan.
Discuss the results you found.

What next?

Making your simulation perfect in the time you have is impossible. Some things you can improve and some you can't.

Things you can fix now

If you found that something didn't work in your simulation (things that don't work as they should are often called 'bugs'!), you could try to fix it.

Things that take too long to fix now

Improvements that have been suggested might take too long to do now. So you can record them as improvements you would like to make.

Activity 4

ASSESSMENT POINTS

▶ Look at your test plan and fix any bugs.
▶ Write a short report to record:
  ● how well your simulation met your success criteria
  ● which bugs you have fixed
  ● what improvements you would like to make if you had more time
  ● Ideas for how you might make these improvements.

Submit your test plan here. **SUBMIT**

Submit your report here. **SUBMIT**

Submit your final simulation here. **SUBMIT**

ASSESS TO PROGRESS

Peer assessment

Self assessment

ASSESS

Wrapping it up

Activity 5

As a class, share some of your ideas for improvements and how you might make them.

Homework

Next lesson you will be revising work you have done on databases and reports. Look back at unit 3 to revise what you know.

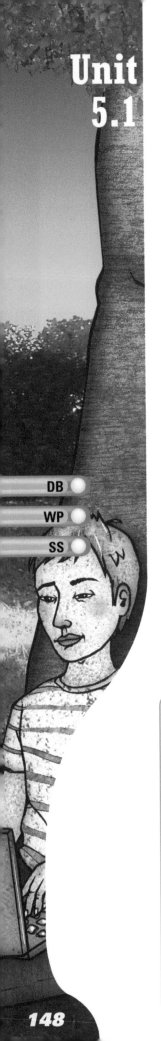

Assessment

IN THIS LESSON

You will:

- Query a large database of cars.
- Produce a report

YOUR CHALLENGE

From: Your head teacher

Subject: Cars and CO_2 emissions

To help improve our carbon footprint, we would like to advise parents which cars are most environmentally friendly. Generally, a car with low CO_2 emissions is more environmentally friendly than one with high CO_2 emissions. I would like you to complete a report for parents that tells them which cars have the lowest CO_2 emissions. Please could you do the following:

1) Query the attached vehicles database to find out which five cars have the lowest CO_2 emissions.
2) Add the five cars you have found to this report.
3) Write whether you think the source is reliable.
4) It has been proposed that SMART cars have the least CO_2 emissions. Use the database to check whether this is the case. Add this to your report.
5) Open this spreadsheet and create a graph showing what methods of transport contribute to CO_2 emissions for the average person. Add this graph to your report along with an explanation of how it shows that it is important to think about CO_2 when choosing a car and why you have chosen this particular type of graph or chart.
6) Add anything you think is appropriate to your report, save it and submit it to me at the end of this lesson.

Thank you

Your head teacher

ASSESSMENT POINTS

	At level 4, you:	At level 5, you:	At level 6, you:
1	Know that data may not be reliable	Can check that data is reasonable and accurate	Understand how to make a range of validation checks as well as visual checks to ensure a valid and reliable data set
2	Can perform simple queries	Can perform more complex queries and know how to get the most effective result	Can perform a complex query efficiently, establishing relevant fields
3	Can represent information graphically showing all the required features and justifying your choice of chart or graph	Can represent information in graphs, charts or tables and in a report, where appropriate, justifying the form of representation and checking the plausibility of your conclusions	Understand how to represent information in different forms and integrate information from a range of ICT tools to produce a more effective solution
4	Understand that the information found can be used to produce a report and recognise the need to check the accuracy of your conclusions		

Activity 1

ASSESSMENT POINTS

Can I do this?

Sort data by column

⬤ DEMO

Filter data

⬤ DEMO

Create a query in a database

⬤ DEMO

Insert a chart

⬤ DEMO

▶ Read the email from your head teacher. Make notes on:
  ⬤ what information you need to find from the database
  ⬤ what you need to produce with this information.

Discuss as a class.

You now have 25 minutes to complete this work and submit it.

Submit your report here **SUBMIT**

Revision point

Creating a query

Look carefully at question 1. What does it require you to do? Which fields are going to be important?

Reliability of data

For question 3, think about:

⬤ what the source is. Is it up-to-date and reliable?

⬤ whether the data looks complete.

Checking a hypothesis

A hypothesis is an idea that needs to be tested out. In question 4, the hypothesis is that SMART cars always have the lowest CO_2 emissions. Look at the vehicles database to find out:

⬤ whether this is true

⬤ if so, what shows this information

⬤ if not, what shows this, and how close the hypothesis is to the truth, e.g. is it completely wrong or almost correct?

Conclusion

Summarise what you have found in terms of:

⬤ data

⬤ how reliable the data is and therefore how reliable your answers are likely to be.

Think of any suggestions you can make for how you could improve your report.

ASSESS TO PROGRESS

Self assessment

⬤ ASSESS

Homework

Next lesson you will be assessed on website design. Look back at Unit 2 to revise what you know.

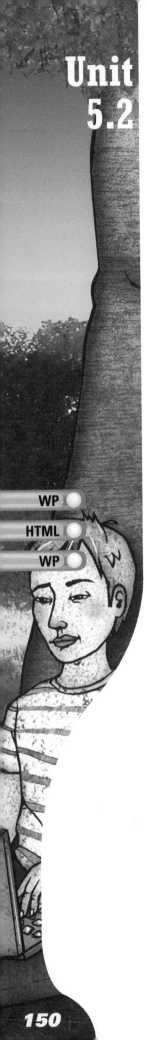

IN THIS LESSON

You will:

- Evaluate a website against success criteria
- Write a report to the designer
- Add content to the website

YOUR CHALLENGE

From: Your head teacher

Subject: Safe collaboration

We need to create a web page for the school about collaborating safely. We will put the video that you created in Unit 1 on to this web page. The audience of the web page is parents and the purpose is to help them learn why collaborative software is important in schools and how we can stay safe.

A website designer has started to create this web page, and has sent his work in for us to check.

Please could you do the following:
1) Open the brief to the school website designer and read it.
2) Now open the website and save it to your user area.
3) Evaluate the website against the brief, thinking about audience and purpose and write a report (using the attached file) to the designer detailing:
   - how well the website matches the brief
   - how appropriate the layout is, what you would change and why
   - how appropriate the design of the website is, what you would change, why and how this could be done efficiently
   - how appropriate the images are, which ones you would change and why.
4) Ask the designer to add some text (either on your report document or in the web page itself using your web editor) describing:
   - why collaborative software is important
   - three potential dangers
   - three ways you can keep safe.
5) Save the changes to your report and submit it to me at the end of this lesson.

Thank you

Your head teacher

Activity 1

ASSESSMENT POINTS

▶ Read the email from your head teacher. Make notes on:
- which documents you need to read
- what you need to produce with this information and how.

Discuss as a class.

You now have 25 minutes to complete this work and submit it.

Can I do this?
Add text

⬤ DEMO

Submit your report here. **SUBMIT** ⬤   Submit your website (if edited) here. **SUBMIT** ⬤

Revision point

- ⬤ Is it fit for audience and purpose?
- ⬤ Does it meet all of the success criteria? If not, how could it be improved?
- ⬤ Remember CHIPS! Give constructive feedback and suggest improvements.

Efficiency

- ⬤ What are the advantages of using webpage templates?

Collaborating safely

- ⬤ Which software tools are useful to help collaboration?
- ⬤ What are the risks of using collaborative software? How can you keep safe?

ASSESS TO PROGRESS

Self assessment

⬤ ASSESS

ASSESSMENT POINTS

	At level 4, you:	At level 5, you:	At level 6, you:
1	Evaluate work against simple, agreed criteria and understand how to improve it	Use simple success criteria that ensure fitness for purpose	Use and review complex success criteria to modify and develop work as it progresses
2		Can use digital communications to share and develop ideas	Know the range of tools available to share and develop ideas automatically
3	Are aware of the risks of sharing personal information and understand how you can help protect yourself	Work in a safe and responsible way when communicating with others	Be responsible, safe and secure in all communications
4		Evaluate a website project with consideration for needs of the audience, expectations and criteria	Evaluate a website with consideration for needs of the audience, expectations, criteria and efficient processes
5	Match presentation and content to purpose	Modify relevant information for a specific purpose, structuring information to meet audience needs	Work independently and efficiently to structure and refine a website for specific audiences and purposes

Homework

Next lesson you will be assessed on sequencing. Look back at Unit 4 to revise what you know.

Assessment

IN THIS LESSON

You will:

- Amend a flow chart of a system
- Add formulae to a simulation
- Amend a macro and add it to your simulation

YOUR CHALLENGE

From: Your head teacher

Subject: Healthy snacks

In Unit 4, you created a system to simulate a security card for school. To encourage pupils to eat more healthily, I would like to introduce a points system. For every healthy snack purchased from the snack machine, the pupil will be awarded 10 points on to his or her card. When the points total is 100, the user will be able to choose a free piece of fruit from the machine.

Please could you do the following:

1) The system needs a flow chart to show the sequence of events in the process. Open this document and save a copy in your user area. Now put the flow chart symbols in the right place and save your changes.
2) Now open this simulation of the system and save it to your user area.
3) In cell B13, add a formula containing an IF statement so that if any points are displayed in cell F12, a message appears saying "Well done for buying a healthy snack", otherwise display "No points yet this visit".
4) In cell B17, add a formula so that if cell F15 is more than 99, a message appears saying "You have earned 100 points – choose your free fruit"; otherwise display "Don't forget you need 100 points to get free fruit!"
5) We have decided to add a 'Check my points' function to the simulation. This will run a macro. Open the macro Beeps on this spreadsheet. This beeps 10 times and gives a message if cell F15 > 99, or gives another message if it is less.
   - Please reduce the number of beeps to 3 as users have found that 10 is too many.
   - Please reduce the pause between beeps to 1 second (instead of 3 seconds).
   - Assign the Beeps macro to the red button 'Check my points'.
   - Test your macro.

Now save your spreadsheet and flow chart and submit them to me at the end of this lesson.

Thank you

Your head teacher

Activity 1

ASSESSMENT POINTS

▶ Read the email from your head teacher. Make notes on:

● which documents you need to look at

● what you need to do and how you will go about this.

Discuss as a class.

You now have 25 minutes to complete this work and submit it.

Submit your flow chart here. **SUBMIT**

Submit your spreadsheet here. **SUBMIT**

Revision point

Sequencing

● Remember it is important to be accurate in your instructions.

● Computers need to be told what to do in exactly the right order..

● You should test your sequence by running through it step by step – or if you are using software such as Visual Basic Editor, you can use the automatic tools to test for errors.

Efficiency

● Remember that there are ways to avoid repeating instructions. Macros can use a loop using, for example:

```
For x = 1 to 3
[instruction here]
Next x
```

Can I do this?

Create a flow chart
○ **DEMO**

Use the IF function
○ **DEMO**

Create repeating code
○ **DEMO**

Use the IF function in a macro
○ **DEMO**

Assign a macro
○ **DEMO**

Run a macro
○ **DEMO**

ASSESSMENT POINTS

	At level 4, you:	At level 5, you:	At level 6, you:
1	Plan sets of instructions	Plan sets of instructions and test and refine them	Break down a problem into smaller sections that can be represented by sub procedures
2	Understand that a set of instructions can be made more efficient by repeating sections	Can write precise and accurate instructions	Structure instructions efficiently to increase flexibility and make testing easier
3			Plan systems by representing them in a diagrammatical form in order to support their development

Homework

Next lesson you will be assessed on investigating and organising data. Look back at Unit 3 to revise what you know.

ASSESS TO PROGRESS

Self assessment

○ **ASSESS**

Assessment

IN THIS LESSON

You will:

- Make changes to a questionnaire
- Plan how you will use your questionnaire
- Make changes to a data entry sheet

YOUR CHALLENGE

From: Your head teacher

Subject: Summer festival

This term we are going to have a summer festival for pupils and parents. As well as being fun and giving parents a chance to see our school, it will also be an opportunity to raise funds to pay for the entertainment on the last day of the festival.

It is important to get as many people along to the festival as possible, both pupils and parents. So we need to find out what people would like and what they would be prepared to buy so that we can organise the events.

We need to know:
- what entertainment people would like
- what pupil work parents would most like to see
- how much money parents are likely to spend at the festival
- what they would like to buy.

Please could you do the following:
1) Open this questionnaire document and save a copy to your user area.
   - Look at the questions on page 1. Are they appropriate? Amend any questions you think could be improved, delete any you think are unnecessary and add any you think are missing.
   - Now look at the questionnaire planning section on page 2. Write down how you could check that the questions on your questionnaire make sense.
   - Write down which groups of people you will send your questionnaire to and how many of each you will send it to.
   - Write down how you will send your questionnaire (e.g. printed, by email) and why.
2) Now open the questionnaire data entry sheet (this is supplied in spreadsheet and database format – choose which you prefer) and save a copy to your user area.
   - Make changes to the questions so they match the questions in your questionnaire.
   - To make the data entry more efficient, add some data validation.
   - Hint: In the spreadsheet version there are suggested answers on the 'Data' sheet; on the database version you should use the wizard to create your answers.

Now save your questionnaire and data entry sheet and submit them to me at the end of this lesson.

Thank you

Your head teacher

WP

DB

SS

Activity 1

▷ Read the email from your head teacher. Make notes on:

- what you need to do on the questionnaire document
- what you need to change on the data entry sheet
- the data validation you might use

Discuss as a class.

You now have 25 minutes to complete this work and submit it.

Submit your questionnaire here. **SUBMIT**

Submit your data entry sheet here. **SUBMIT**

Revision point

Can I do this?

Add validation to a database

DEMO

Add validation to a spreadsheet

DEMO

Closed and open questions

- Closed questions be answered with a simple yes or no.
- Open questions might be answered with all kinds of responses, making analysing data difficult. You can overcome this with a list of possible responses.
- You should always try to get some of your target audience to read through your questionnaire to check that the questions make sense to them.

Samples

Choose a representative sample to make sure that the answers are fair.

Data validation

It is always possible that someone will put the wrong data into the answer, making it difficult to analyse. Avoid this by adding data validation to ensure that people put in answers that are in the right format and are valid. Think about:

- ways to make sure people enter the right type of entry
- ways to help people check from a range of options,

ASSESS TO PROGRESS

Self assessment

ASSESS

ASSESSMENT POINTS

	At level 4, you:	At level 5, you:	At level 6, you:
1	Know how to identify the key data you need to solve a problem	Can identify the key data and ICT tools you need to solve a problem	
2	Identify closed questions	Identify closed and open questions and know what questions are appropriate to the audience	Use closed and open questions effectively and frame questions so that they can be entered efficiently
3		Collect relevant feedback and act on it	
4			Establish validation checks to ensure that data is valid and reliable

Techniques

DATABASE

FILE MANAGEMENT

INTERNET

SOUND AND VIDEO TOOLS

SPREADSHEET

WEB PAGE CREATION SOFTWARE

WORD PROCESSING

Index

Pearson Education
Edinburgh Gate
Harlow
Essex
CM20 2JE

ISBN: 978-1-4058-6456-5

Illustrations by Annabelle Hartmann
Indexed by Indexing Specialists (UK) Ltd

Printed in Great Britain

The publisher's policy is to use paper manufactured from sustainable forests

Acknowledgments
The Publisher is grateful to the following for their permission to reproduce copyright material: Blue Peter Time Capsule story, source: www.bbcnews.co.uk, January 2000.

The publisher would like to thank the following for their kind permission to reproduce their photographs:

(Key: b-bottom; c-centre; l-left; r-right; t-top)

Alamy Images: Arco Images GmbH 69tr; D. Hurst 80; Jeff Gynane 38; Horizon International Images Limited 68 (background); Natural Visions 69cr; Stefan Sollfors 76, 113; BBC Photo Library: 39tl, 39tr; Getty Images: Aurora / Peter Essick 69tl; iStockphoto: Alohaspirit 68 (inset); Franck Boston 8-9; Koksharov Dmitry 47b, 54, 61, 63; Eric Isselée 92, 101, 105; Jane Norton 20br; PA Photos: PA Archive / PA Photos 69b; Pearson Education Ltd: 11, 15, 19, 20bl, 21, 41, 55, 71, 117, 121, 122; PunchStock: Digital Vision 97; Rex Features: CSU Archives / Everett Collection 39b

All other images © Pearson Education

Picture Research by: Louise Edgeworth

Every effort has been made to trace the copyright holders and we apologise in advance for any unintentional omissions. We would be pleased to insert the appropriate acknowledgement in any subsequent edition of this publication.

Microsoft, Word, Excel, PowerPoint, Access and Internet Explorer are trademarks of the Microsoft Corporation.
Dreamweaver is trademark of Macromedia.
WebPlus is a trademark of Serif Europe Ltd.

Every effort has been made to trace the copyright holders and we apologise in advance for any unintentional omissions. We would be pleased to insert the appropriate acknowledgement in any subsequent edition of this publication.